Women
with
Autism

Claire Jack

First published in 2021
by Casacat Press Ltd.
272 Bath Street
Glasgow, G2 4JR
UK

Disclaimer
Whilst I have drawn on my experiences of working with women with
autism, their stories have been mixed together, changed and otherwise
disguised in order to protect their identities. No single person has been
depicted in their entirety.

ISBN: 978-1-8384961-9-7

DEDICATION

To Bryan, Duncan & Simon

CONTENTS

Preface   *vii*

Note on terminology   *x*

Acknowledgements   *xi*

1   Introduction   1

2   What is Autism Spectrum Disorder?   9

3   Do I Have Autism?   17

4   How do I get a Diagnosis (and do I Need One)?   32

5   I have Autism! So, What Now?   49

6   Imagining an Authentic Life   62

7   Developing Strategies   81

8   Embracing Your Special Interests   90

9   Pursuing an Authentic Career   97

10   Becoming Your Authentic Social Self   104

11   Autism and Gendered Discourses   118

12   Self-Care and Emotional Regulation   127

13   Making Sense of the Past   154

14   Your Autism Superpowers   166

15   You're More Than a Diagnosis   175

16   Accessing Support   182

17   Going Forwards   191

References   *193*

PREFACE

As my legs buckled under me, I lunged for a seat, leaving my elderly mum to deal with the doctor's receptionist. By the time I made it back to the sanctuary of my own home, my partner found me sobbing in my bed.

I explained about the change in plans that had taken course during the day: the unnecessary trip to yet another supermarket because mum needed a particular brand of tea; the unexpected blood tests which added half an hour on to the doctor's appointment; her incessant chatter with half a dozen people which meant there was no way I was going to fit a gym workout in. This was day five of my mum's relocation 100 miles south to be nearer to me and I couldn't cope with the chaos.

Cocooned in the peace of a therapist's chair a couple of days later, I described the mess and chaos that had accompanied my mum's move and that had pushed my anxiety levels, which were fairly bad even on a good day, through the roof. I explained that my carefully constructed daily routine which helped to keep my anxiety levels at bay, was out the window and how I was experiencing burnout after less than a week of mum's relocation.

After listening patiently, the counsellor said, "Have you ever considered that you might be on the autistic spectrum?"

"No..." I replied. Frankly, it wasn't a thought that had ever occurred to me. My first response was to feel insulted. Yes, I was slightly obsessive about things matching, had regular meltdowns when my plans were disrupted in the most minor ways and could remember car number plates from 10 years ago. But autistic? I didn't think so.

And yet, in the following days, I began to wonder whether the problems which I'd experienced my entire life could, in fact, be due to autism. Going right back to my earliest childhood, I'd been described as "highly sensitive," "withdrawn," and plain old-fashioned "weird." My numerous phobias, need for order, social anxiety, meltdowns, complete absorption in subjects and extreme auditory and kinesthetic sensitivity all fitted with "autism." But I didn't fit what I thought was the autistic profile. I was determined to find out more, though and I began to research women and Autism Spectrum Disorder (ASD).

During this time, I felt as if I was emerging from a thick fog. I began to tentatively look at different phases of my life through the lens of someone with autism and came up with new interpretations which fitted so closely that, at times, it was overwhelming.

Discovering I have autism has completely changed my life;

from making sense of a childhood in which I never felt like a child, to providing an explanation for the difficulties I experienced in every job and relationship I had ever been in, to helping me realise I wasn't selfish and demanding simply because I had to construct my life in a particular way. Autism has become a significant part of my story which has helped make sense of the other parts.

So many women with autism live their lives by camouflaging[1], or masking, and becoming all things to all people that, in the process, they have lost a sense of self. If that rings true for you, I invite you to imagine a future where you can be true to yourself as you move towards authenticity. I have drawn together everything I have learned about myself and from working with inspiring, brave, creative women who have made the journey towards living a life which meets their needs and I'm so happy to be able to share that knowledge with you.

A NOTE ON TERMINOLOGY

In line with DSM-5, Autism Spectrum Disorder can be subdivided into Levels 1, 2 and 3. People with level 1 autism are assessed as being able to lead an independent life, or manage with minimal support. People with level 2 ASD require substantial support and people with level 3 ASD may have severe deficits in verbal and communication skills, learning difficulties and require very substantial support[2]. This book is aimed towards women who would qualify for a diagnosis of Level 1 Autism Spectrum Disorder (or Asperger's Syndrome, a diagnostic category which existed as a distinct category in the DSM between 1994 and 2013, and which has since been incorporated into Autism Spectrum Disorder). There is ongoing debate about the use of terms such as high-functioning, or Level 1 autism, given the value laden nature of these terms. Whilst I sympathise with this perspective, in terms of ensuring this book is accessible to those people for whom it will be most helpful, it is aimed towards women with level 1/ high-functioning autism. These terms may be used during this book.

ACKNOWLEDGMENTS

The inspiration for this book came to me as a result of working with my clients who shared their experiences with me. Whilst all names, details and stories have been significantly changed and amalgamated in order to protect their identities, I would like to thank those women who have contributed to my knowledge of what it is to be a woman with autism. I'm very grateful to Katie Nicol, who has been a great sounding board about both women and autism and my writing experience over many cups of coffee. Thanks to Bryan Drummond for his constant support, belief in me and practical help which has given me the time, space and confidence to write. To Duncan Jack for listening carefully, asking all the right questions and encouraging me in terms of getting the book out there. And to Simon Jack for his unwavering enthusiasm and support during the writing process.

1 INTRODUCTION

I swayed to the soft music on the television, lost in the test card which was projected at the end of programming, immersing myself in the bright image of a girl and a clown playing noughts and crosses, all neatly contained within a geometric pattern. I'd been there some time – I could happily keep this up as long as the test card was on, which was a long time in 1970s Britain – when my mum told me we were going out. Frustration and anger bubbled up in my four year old's body. How dare she interrupt my interpretive dance session? Especially when all she had to offer was a trip to the supermarket, with its harsh lights, clattering trolleys and an incessant onslaught of people. My feeling of oneness with the world came to an abrupt end.

My authentic self, the one who could sit for hours with a cat, or looking through a book, or drawing a picture, remained hidden during the supermarket trip. When anyone approached us in the shop, I would position myself behind mum, pulling her skirt around me, to protect myself from the intrusion of having my head patted or my chin grabbed between a forefinger and thumb, whose smell and sensation I was acutely aware of. "She's shy", the old ladies would say, and I would hide my face deeper into mum's soft skirt, relieved that I'd got rid of the intruder.

Mum was fairly patient, I don't think there's much you can do about a kid glaring at people and hiding when you're holding a baby and trying to have a conversation, until one day she told me off. "Smile", she said through gritted teeth, "Just smile at people when they talk. Say hello. You can't keep doing this!". And so, ever obedient, I made a conscious effort to smile when people approached. Saying hello was too much, but I learned that a smile will do, especially if I put up with my head being patted, despite feeling the sensation resonate harshly throughout my body. I had no interest in being liked or receiving attention, but I was terrified of making mum angry.

As I got older, I realised that *my self* was not an attractive option for many people, particularly those who came into contact with me on a superficial level. I was quiet, shy, sensitive, bookish and introverted. I wasn't girly enough, or charming enough, or cute enough or playful enough.

Throughout the years, I learned other skills which allowed me to pass as fairly normal; some of which I didn't pick up until well into adulthood. These included: asking people a question about themselves; showing an interest in some really dull conversations; making eye contact; and forcing myself to say something, even if it was just one word and even if I felt like vomiting as it came out of my mouth, in a group conversation. I developed a checklist of what to say and when to say it. If I was stumped after one social meeting, or said and did the wrong thing, I made a conscious effort never to repeat my mistake. I worried about meeting new people, I worried during conversations with those I knew and I ruminated for hours on end after being in a group of people when I thought I'd "got it wrong". But my checklist gave me something to hold onto when I was in company.

And so, I got by. Not by bringing my true self to the table, but by camouflaging who I was. Where is the harm in that, you might ask? Surely, we all have to mask aspects of our personality as we go through life, whether or not we have autism? To some extent, this is correct and research shows that neurotypical people also employ camouflaging strategies[3]. The harm appears to be related to the *degree* to which women with autism camouflage[4,5,6]. When you have autism, you are *constantly* adapting to a situation which inherently doesn't work for you because it doesn't make any room for your needs and wants. Consistently masking is exhausting, depressing and anxiety-provoking.

The harmful effects of camouflaging are also related to the fact that only one way of being is deemed "right" and the autism way is deemed "wrong". When you are forced to buy into this perspective, you grow up with a lack of self-acceptance and self-worth. You're not just "shy", you're *too* shy. You're not just "direct", you're *too* direct. You're not just "enthusiastic", you're *too* enthusiastic. Too tantrummy, too obsessive, too blunt, too sensitive…and the list goes on. There is a strong judgement inherent in these beliefs that *your authentic self* is not acceptable. And so, at the same time as you're learning to smile, ask questions, put up with people touching your face and stifling your boredom when you're subjected to small talk, you learn to hide, suppress and deny those parts of your personality which (from what you have learned about the world) you assume other people consider unacceptable, until you consider them to be unacceptable, too. After years of internalising the messages around you, you come to the conclusion that not only are you too much, you're also not enough.

Judging yourself as "not good enough", because you're different to many other people, means that you stop listening to and recognising what you need to feel fulfilled in life. It means making choices which don't fit with your values or meet your needs. And it means that you become fearful of revealing your wonderful and unique personality to the rest of the world because you are scared of rejection and judgement.

Until you can accept who you are and value yourself deeply enough to bring your true, authentic self to others, you will experience an incongruence between your values and your actions. When you keep acting in a certain way because you think you *should*, even when it feels wrong to you, you will feel anxious and disillusioned. When you fail to get in touch with what excites and nurtures you, because those things are considered weird and unnecessary, you will feel unfulfilled. When you cannot reveal who you are and what matters to you, you will feel frustrated and unseen.

Taking the first tentative steps towards authenticity involves getting in touch with who you are and what you need and want out of life. When you've spent a lifetime being all things to all people, this can be particularly challenging. It's a tough call for anybody and especially challenging for someone who is starting from a different point to most people; the point of being neurodivergent in a neurotypical world.

Struggling to fit into the world, and denying your authentic self, can cause self-dislike and low self-esteem and there is a strong link between autism and mental health issues, including anxiety and depression[7]. Consistently masking your true self goes beyond putting on a cloak of normality in the company of others to a lack of self-acceptance which kicks in even when it's just you on you. Is there a space where you can reveal and accept your true self *to* yourself, or have you reached a point where you devalue yourself, because you don't seem to fit with a social norm? Have those messages from those around you reached a point where they have become your core beliefs? If your choices flow from this point, it's difficult to be authentic even with yourself.

Becoming authentic, then, isn't just about revealing your true self to others, it is about learning to love and accept yourself *as you are*. It is about discovering what you love in life, what nurtures your mind, body and soul and having the conviction to pursue those things. It is about valuing yourself enough to meet your needs and wants. And it is about recognising the validity of those needs and wants for *you*; no matter how different they may seem to most of the people around you. If what you truly desire is to live separately from your partner because you need space, that's *ok*. If you want to avoid a family party because you know it will make you feel ill afterwards for two days, that's ok too. If you want to work on a farm looking after horses instead of using your law degree, you can go for it! No matter how long you've been forcing yourself to show up in a way which conflicts with your authentic self, you can create the change.

My own journey towards authenticity hasn't been easy. It's involved removing myself from people who cause me stress. It has involved courage in getting out there and being open about the struggles I have faced with anxiety, depression and addiction. I've had to stop hiding in the shadows and make myself heard and seen, no matter how much I dislike doing so. But the benefits of becoming more authentic have far outweighed the difficulties and my life has more meaning and purpose than I even knew was possible. The anxiety which has plagued me since the age of five has, finally, become more manageable than I ever imagined. Rather than view myself as defective, difficult or demanding, I view myself as having certain needs. Embracing and revealing my true self is the most enjoyable thing I've ever done. It's fun to rediscover the things that make me tick, and to recognise those things as a need and not an indulgence. It's healing to be patient with myself, to have an afternoon nap when I need to, to take the pressure off myself to socialise and to embrace those aspects of my work which are creative and focused. It's inspiring to imagine a future where I can be myself and surround myself with other people who are loving and accepting.

Becoming authentically autistic is a journey and through this book, I will be there beside you as you take your first steps, from exploring whether or not you may have autism to what to expect if you pursue a formal diagnosis. The early days of coming to terms with a diagnosis can be confusing and fearful, and I will help you identify some of the issues which might come up for you at this time. Defining what authenticity looks and feels like to you is an exciting prospect and I will help you explore the choices and opportunities available to you. We'll look together at what you need to do to value and accept your inner self, whilst respecting your personal values and needs for safety and privacy. This book will help you celebrate your uniqueness, and to become comfortable with who you are.

I've provided you with self-development exercises throughout this book which will help you identify and keep a note of the strategies you adopt as you pursue a more authentic life. This book isn't just designed to provide information. I want you to use it as a thought provoking, practical resource and make sure you take it with you on your journey towards authenticity.

2 WHAT IS AUTISM SPECTRUM DISORDER?

Before going any further, it's useful to have a knowledge of what exactly Autism Spectrum Disorder is. ASD is a *neurodevelopmental disorder* ("developmental" disorders are generally apparent by the age of two or earlier, although autism may go undetected until far later and sometimes not until adulthood) which causes difficulties in social interaction and communication and is characterised by restricted and repetitive patterns of behaviour[8]. It is considered a *spectrum disorder* because it encompasses a wide range of symptoms which vary between individuals, meaning that one person with autism will present in a very different way to another. However, whether someone is at one end of the spectrum and has high intellectual capabilities and reasonable communication skills or they are at the other end of the spectrum and have a learning disability and an inability to communicate effectively, it is believed that the underlying causes of their condition are the same.

People with Asperger's Syndrome, Level 1 or "high-functioning" Autism Spectrum Disorder are of average, or above average, intelligence. Whilst they may function independently and may be able to hold down a job and lead a full life, they display symptoms such as obsessive and rigid thinking, problems with social interactions, difficulty recognising faces and non-verbal communication and a difficulty with working out other people's intentions. Many people with autism feel easily confused and overwhelmed socially and can develop anxiety and depression as a result of trying to cope with a difficult world. Being level 1, or "high-functioning", doesn't mean that life is easy.

What causes autism?

Autism does not have a single cause and it is likely that there are a number of factors, including genetic and environmental factors, which increase the likelihood of autism.

We've known since the 1990s that genes play a role in autism. In the biggest study of its kind, involving analysis of more than 35000 people, including nearly 12000 people with autism, researchers identified 102 genes which were associated with brain development or brain function[9]. 49 of these genes were linked to other developmental delays in addition to ASD. Research into twins has shown that autism has a strong genetic component and may run in families[10]. Whilst we know there is a genetic risk for autism[11], we're still unsure as to the mechanisms involved[12].

Another causal factor in autism may be the health of the

autistic person's mother. Research has shown that the mother's health, and even her own personal trauma history, may increase her chances of having a child with autism. One study showed that women who had experienced the highest levels of abuse were 60% more likely to have a child with autism[13]. The link between earlier life abuse and having a child with autism may be explained by the fact that the mother's physical and mental makeup has been fundamentally changed as a result of childhood abuse, including alterations to the mother's Hypothalamic Pituitary Adrenal (HPA) axis[14,15,16]. The HPA axis is associated with our response to stress and the initiation of our "fight or flight" response. It is suggested that dysregulation of a mother's HPA axis may affect the developing fetal brain[17] and a dysregulated HPA axis is also more common in people with autism[18].

Childhood abuse may also lead to changes in a mother's immune system, which may increase her likelihood of having a child with autism[19]. During pregnancy, a mother's inflammation levels (which are linked to immune function) can affect the development of the child's brain and some researchers suggest that maternal inflammation and immune function may cause autism[20,21,22]. Androgens, another group of hormones which are associated with high levels of psychosocial stress[23], have also been associated with autism[24]. Another factor which might explain the link between a mother's childhood abuse and an increased likelihood that she will have a child with autism is because she may herself have had undiagnosed autism or another mental illness/ disorder, given the high overlap between autism and other mental disorders[25,26,27].

Some recent studies have proposed a link between women's health and diet and their likelihood of having a child with autism, including one study which showed that women who took folic acid and iron during pregnancy reduced their likelihood of having a child with autism and intellectual disabilities by up to 30%[28].

The shift towards exploring genetic and biological causes of autism represents a departure from earlier attempts to explain autism as a result of upbringing and, in particular, "detached mothering", a view first proposed by the psychiatrist, Leo Kanner[29]. This view was popularised in the 1960s by psychologist Bruno Bettleheim, who coined the phrase "refrigerator mothering"[30]. From the late 1960s, parents of children with autism increasingly rejected the nature of their parenting as a cause for their children's autism[31]. Today, biological explanations for autism are generally accepted by those affected by autism and by the professional healthcare sector.

Autism as a male condition

We now know that women and men experience autism differently, and present with different symptoms. However, it is only in recent years that researchers and healthcare professionals have become aware of these differences. Prior to this, our knowledge of autism was based almost exclusively on the male experience of autism. The reasons for this are rooted in the original identification of autism as a male condition and subsequent research, which has had a male bias.

The term "autism" was first used in 1908 by Eugen Bleuler to describe a subset of schizophrenic patients who were especially withdrawn and self-absorbed[32]. However, it was not used as a diagnostic term until 1943 by the child psychiatrist, Leo Kanner[33]. Kanner's research into 11 children, who he identified as intelligent and who had a strong desire to be alone and displayed restricted interests, only included 3 girls in the sample. The following year, Austrian physician Hans Asperger also used case studies to research autism and his sample only included boys. In fact, Asperger concluded that "the autistic personality is an extreme variant of male intelligence" and that women and girls could not have autism (although he later changed his mind)[34]. Historically, therefore, diagnostic criteria have been based on studies predominantly or exclusively based on male experience.

The "extreme male brain" theory[35], which proposes that autistic people process the world through a "male" lens and have primarily stereotypically male interests, may also have influenced clinicians in terms of considering autism as a primarily "male" condition, and has influenced diagnostic criteria[36]. Research into autism has predominantly continued to focus on men and, in the case of neuroimaging research, there is an ascertainment bias (meaning that males are specifically selected in favour of females as research subjects) of up to 15:1[37].

A combination of the above factors led to the belief that far more men than women have autism, which, in turn, has led to the under-diagnosis of women. Ongoing research has challenged these assumptions and has revealed that significantly higher numbers of girls and women have autism than previously thought. In 2009 a study in England found that 1.8% of men and boys were diagnosed with autism, compared to 0.2% of women and girls[39]. More recent studies have revealed smaller male-female ratios[39] with one recent review suggesting that males are approximately three times more likely to have ASD than females[40].

Another reason for the under-diagnosis of women, and the perpetuation of the idea that autism is a male condition, is because of the differences between male and female presentation of autistic symptoms, which can make diagnosis problematic (especially given the fact that diagnostic criteria are based primarily on male experience). Girls, for instance, report more sensory symptoms and fewer socio-communication difficulties than boys[41] and their special, restricted interests often appear to be more "normal" than those of boys[42], meaning they can be more easily missed by caregivers and healthcare professionals. Girls and women are more likely to hide, or mask, their symptoms and become extremely adept at doing so, which also contributes to under-diagnosis of females[43].

Consequently, women and girls with autism may not receive a diagnosis and related support. A lack of appropriate support could have a negative effect on their mental health and well-being[44]. Because many women are so successful as presenting as socially competent, they tend to be diagnosed later in life than men and are less likely to be referred for clinical assessment[45]. The situation is beginning to change, however, and researchers have increasingly become aware that autism often goes undiagnosed in girls, partly due to the fact that their symptoms are different to boys[46], as is their ability to mask their symptoms[47].

Although girls face many similar social communication problems to boys, including difficulty with reading facial expressions and working out the intentions of other people, suffering from overwhelm when presented with too much information at one time and becoming exhausted in social situations, they tend to be more driven to interact socially and put considerable effort into learning how to do so. They learn how to make eye contact, smile and what to say when they meet someone. Girls often create a checklist of socially acceptable behaviours which they can refer to. They tend to display more of a need than boys to make friends and they put all their incredible learning abilities into working out how to do this.

Keeping those friends, especially when things get complicated, can be difficult as is the whole process of being sociable but many girls and women can, at least, "pass" as being as reasonably sociable.

The fact that girls with autism have this drive to be sociable suggests that it stems from the inherent differences between boys and girls in terms of their need for social relationships. When you look at any groups of neurotypical girls and boys, they interact differently and girls appear to be more socially oriented than boys[48,49]. From birth, girls are more interested in human faces[50,51] and appear to behave more prosocially than boys[52]. They also show an interest in one-to-one time with other girls, whereas boys are more interested in playing in groups, and girls display increased levels of social complexity at an earlier age than boys[53]. More areas of girls' brains, including the cerebral cortex, which is responsible for memory, attention, thought and language, are dedicated to verbal functions and girls have higher levels of oxytocin and serotonin, which tend to make them calmer than boys[54].

Perhaps a useful way to think of this is that, although you share an autistic brain with men who have autism, you are female, with a brain which is influenced by your gender. It makes complete sense that men and women will experience autism differently when we take into account the inherent differences in their make up.

3 DO I HAVE AUTISM?

"Do I have autism?", is a hugely significant question. If you're asking this question by the time you've reached adulthood, you will probably have spent a lifetime with a sense that you were "different" to most of the other women you know and feeling that life has been difficult, despite your best efforts.

Perhaps you're in the very early stages of trying to establish whether or not you have autism, or you may have received a diagnosis of autism and are interested in finding out what this means for you. Whatever stage you are at in your journey, this question, and the answers which arise from it, can be life changing.

You may initially find yourself asking this question because:

- A therapist has suggested to you that you may have autism.

- A friend or family member has suggested to you that you may have autism.

- You've experienced difficulties in certain areas of your life and your research into your symptoms has led you to questioning whether ASD might be the reason.
- You have a child who has been diagnosed with autism which has led you to question whether you have autism.

After a lifetime of struggle and, if you're like many women with autism, trying to be something you're inherently not, the question, "Do I have autism?" carries huge weight. Addressing this question has the potential to help you make sense of your past and define your future. When you achieve a greater awareness of why things happened as a child or in younger adulthood, it provides you with a greater understanding of why you are the way you are today. This is important on several levels. Understanding your past can help you to understand how and why you repeat particular patterns of behaviour. Awareness can help you come to terms with aspects of your life which are tinged with regret or a sense of shame. Sadly, many women look back on their difficulties and feel bad about themselves for finding it so hard to cope.

Awareness is also empowering as you move forwards in life. If you understand why you have always been drawn to certain ways of acting and thinking, you can be aware of what makes you tick as you continue your journey. This awareness provides an opportunity to start adjusting your routines, your relationships and your life goals with respect to the fact that your brain works in a particular way. Instead of keeping being that square peg trying to fit into the round hole, you can work on creating a square which neatly fits your peg. Accepting that you're a certain way gives you the permission you need to start living a life which feels more "right".

However, even asking this question in the first place, let alone finding the answer to it, can be a very scary prospect. Unless you already know someone with autism, you probably don't know much about it and the word "disorder" doesn't sound particularly inviting. What you do know about autism may come from films and books depicting people with ASD and related learning difficulties, such as *I am Sam*, or Savant traits, such as Dustin Hoffman's character in *Rainman*. Autism is a spectrum disorder; and the spectrum is huge. Whilst there's no one way to experience autism, and we need to recognise and celebrate all forms of neurodiversity, if you're a woman with level 1 Autism who has made it to adulthood and who may have held down a job, been a parent and fulfilled other roles which most people consider "normal", you may find it difficult to identify with what you currently know about autism. We grow up with a societal pressure to feel "normal" and women with autism go to extraordinary lengths to hide their differences. So being presented with an opportunity to be diagnosed with a condition which identifies you as neurodivergent can be terrifying.

My first reactions to the suggestion that I might be on the

spectrum were a mix of feeing insulted, excited and ashamed. One day, I would wake up thinking, "Hooray! This explains *everything*!". And the next, I would feel embarrassed that there was something "wrong" with me. In my most paranoid moments, I wondered why the therapist had suggested ASD in the first place. She'd studied women with autism for a dissertation. Did she just have an agenda of suggesting that pretty much every woman who walked through her door had autism? At times, it felt like an insulting label to me and I oscillated between feeling optimistic and relieved that I had "something" to feeling desolate that I was destined to be odd. I couldn't get the stereotypes out of my head and felt strongly that I didn't fit with them.

Rosa described a similar response to being told by a therapist that she might have autism. "I didn't have much of a rapport with her [the therapist] and it felt like she was saying something horrible to me, like it wasn't coming from a good place".

For Leona, the experience was also initially viewed in a negative light. "My friend, whose brother has autism, asked me whether I had ever considered that I might be autistic. I was really quite shocked and thought she was trying to put me down".

Like me, Rosa and Leona's knowledge of autism came from representations in film and tv and from hearing occasional news stories about "Savants", who are autistic people with learning difficulties and are particularly gifted in particular areas. It's not surprising that so many of us react negatively to the suggestion that we may have autism when there is so little awareness of how it affects women, particularly.

Not everyone experiences a negative reaction, instead experiencing a sense of overwhelming relief almost instantly.

For Josie, the suggestion that she might have autism, initially from a friend whose child had autism, was "like a lightbulb going on. I felt so relieved that there might be an explanation for why I was the way I was".

Diana, who had previously been diagnosed with Bipolar Disorder, a diagnosis which she never felt fitted her, was similarly relieved when her psychiatrist suggested that she may have autism. "For the first time, it seemed like something made sense. It made sense to me that there was something different in my brain which made me think and act like I do. I felt a huge weight off my shoulders".

Exploring whether or not you have autism and feeling a lack of identification with people with autism (based on your existing knowledge), is particularly difficult for women due to the simple reason that diagnostic criteria are heavily weighted towards men. This means that, if you do an autism test on the internet, which is an obvious starting point for many people, you may score as "borderline" at best. On a far more serious note, it means that if and when you contact your primary healthcare provider to explore the possibility of being referred for diagnosis, you may find it very difficult to be referred for psychiatric assessment. If you get as far as the psychiatrist's door, unless they have a knowledge of how autism affects women, you may fail to receive a diagnosis of autism.

Exercise:

Get nice and comfortable and make sure you have some time alone to experience the following exercise.

Ask yourself the question, "Do I have autism?".

How do you feel mentally and physically when you ask yourself this question? Any and all responses are totally valid. Just let your emotions come to the surface and name them. Identifying what you are feeling at the start of your journey will increase your awareness of those issues which you might find difficult, and prepare you to navigate these issues. It will also help you to identify the positive feelings which arise as you explore this question.

Taking the test

There are several autism tests which you can take online which might be your first step in answering whether or not you have autism. Because of the weighting towards male autism, you may or may not get a conclusive answer on these diagnostic tests. It should also be noted that, just as with the checklist below, these are not the same as seeing a psychiatrist for a full diagnosis. They are simply a starting point to help you establish whether or not autism fits with your symptoms. If you find yourself identifying with the majority of symptoms on the checklist, you may have ASD (although, it should be noted that many of the symptoms overlap with other conditions and a professional opinion can you help you establish whether your symptoms are autism related).

The checklist I have developed below is an amalgamation of conducting research into women with autism and consulting a range of diagnostic tests. I have divided the checklist into sections, with a brief overview in each. Take some time to work through the checklist. You may find yourself identifying with more symptoms in one section or another and, if you have autism, you will probably find yourself identifying with many of the symptoms.

Social symptoms

Women with autism often struggle socially, feeling uncomfortable in social situations, finding it hard to work out people's motives and feeling exhausted and overwhelmed after socially interacting. They may face confusion and misunderstand what is being said. Following social cues is difficult, as is establishing eye contact. On the flip side, they tend to be excellent at mimicking other people and learning to "pass" as normal.

It can be difficult for a woman with autism to establish whether she has ASD or is socially anxious. The following list may be helpful in helping you work out whether autism may explain some of your social difficulties.

Have you, or do you currently find yourself:

- Being bullied by other people

- Being sexually abused

- Being emotionally abused

- Monitoring your behaviour and responses in social situations

- Feeling confused in social situations

- Feeling exhausted after a group meeting/party

- Fluid concept of sexuality

- Drinking to cope with social situations

- Feeling tongue tied in social situations

- Disliking "small talk"

- Favouring one-on-one relationships to group relationships

- Wanting to talk about issues/ hobbies you are passionate about

- Needing a "checklist" for what to say when you meet new people

- Feeling awkward and out of place

- Putting in effort to say and do the right thing

- Needing time alone to recharge

- Finding it hard to understand and follow directions

- Difficulty in making and maintaining eye contact

- Desiring a very few close friends rather than a large group of friends

- Being happy to go long periods without catching up with friends
- Finding it hard to identify with other women

Sensory

Many women with autism experience issues with "filtering" sensory input, which can lead to an overload of information and the need to focus intently on one thing in order to avoid being overloaded. People with ASD may be highly sensitive and over-responsive to sounds, sights, smells, touch, and tastes. Many women are particularly sensitive to the feeling of clothes and makeup, pulling off clothing tags and opting for comfortable clothes over fashionable clothes and shoes. Many of my clients report being unable to stand high pitched noises or the loud noises and lights of a concert. Issues with sleeping and a heightened sensitivity to quiet noises at night time is common. Some people with autism experience a reduced response to sensory stimuli, which may make them seek out sensory experiences to satisfy their need to experience things on a sensory level.

Have you, or do you currently find yourself:

- Disliking tags in clothes
- Being sensitive to high pitched noises
- Finding some sensations (such as wool or nylon) difficult to cope with

- Disliking tight or uncomfortable clothes or shoes
- Choosing practical clothes over "attractive" clothes
- Disliking feeling of foundation or lipstick
- Disliking feeling of substances on fingertips (eg: fruit dirt, roughness)
- Being affected by bright lights
- Issues with sleeping and sensitivity to noise at night
- Feeling overwhelmed in supermarkets/ shopping stores
- Feeling overwhelmed or disliking being hugged/ kissed by acquaintances
- Desire for spatial organisation, such as colour coordination
- Disliking loud environments (such as concerts)
- Having a strong reaction to certain scents (such as perfume)
- Failing to notice things in your environment
- Strong aversions to types of foods

Emotional

Women with Autism Spectrum Disorder often have difficulties with emotional regulation. Many of the day-to-day things which are comparatively manageable for many people can be extremely hard for women with autism. Social situations can bring on feelings of panic, confusion and extreme exhaustion afterwards. Day-to-day demands, like being interrupted in the middle of a task and having to readjust one's plans can lead to feelings of deep anger and frustration. In addition to finding it hard to cope with a range of situations, women with autism may find that they respond in deeply empathic to difficulties faced by others, but have problems in processing or expressing their reaction. Women with autism may find it hard to communicate their needs, generally, and keep things bottled up until they experience a meltdown.

Have you, or do you currently find yourself:
- Becoming emotionally overwhelmed
- Feeling exhausted or "burnt out"
- "Acting out" or having extreme emotional reactions (meltdowns)
- Becoming emotionally confused & not knowing how to react
- Being diagnosed with anxiety or depression
- Feeling a deep physical response to someone else's distress
- Having difficulty in processing or expressing emotional response
- Finding it easier to shut off from other people's distress
- Having difficulty in expressing needs
- Feeling confused or disoriented
- Having poor emotional regulation
- Feeling extreme anxiety when routines/ plans are changed
- Desire to be alone to emotionally recharge
- Experiencing an eating disorder

- Engaging in "black and white" or "all or nothing" thinking
- "Escaping" through music, real or imagine

Repetitive behaviours

People with autism may have a strong desire to do things repetitively, to stick to one way of doing things and may face difficulties when their routines are interrupted. Everyday tasks may have to be carried out in the same way, over and over, in order to avoid feelings of anxiety.

Have you, or do you currently find yourself:

- "Stimming" (for instance, rocking back & forwards, pulling hair, picking scabs, rubbing feet together)
- Having "rituals" that you need to follow
- Carrying out tasks in the same manner and feeling distressed if you can't repeat this process
- Listening to same song over and over again

Focus, "obsessions" & organisational behaviour

Women with ASD tend to be very focused on their interests and passions. They can become extremely interested in a hobby or their work, sometimes to the exclusion of other interests and activities. They are often very good at conducting research and engaging in careers which involve a high degree of organisational behaviour – such as cataloguing and collecting – and often describe themselves as being quite "obsessive" in nature.

Have you, or do you currently find yourself:

- Experiencing "obsessions" with a celebrity or band
- Experiencing obsessive behaviour towards a romantic "crush" or partner
- Experiencing an intense level of focus on your partner in romantic relationship
- Having an inability to switch easily from one task to another and back again
- Displaying a strong desire to engage in your hobbies, work or interests
- Experiencing difficulties when plans are changed with little or no notice
- Having problems adapting to change
- Being intensely passionate about hobbies, interests or causes
- Having difficulties when your routines are disrupted
- Experiencing difficulty establishing "day to day" routines when there are more interesting things to do

Noticing details

People with ASD often notice things that other people tend to miss, and may find themselves noticing patterns and creating systems from seemingly random information.

Have you, or do you currently find yourself:

- Noticing and remembering car number plates

- Noticing patterns in numbers

- Picking out sounds/ details in music

- Noticing the detailed picture rather than the "big picture"

- Sometimes missing details that others would notice

Childhood

Autism doesn't appear out of nowhere. It is a developmental disorder and, if you have ASD, the types of difficulties you currently face will be identifiable in your childhood, even if you and those around you weren't fully aware of the issues you faced at the time. Talking to a parent is a useful first step in establishing the types of behaviours they may have noticed in you which they felt were different, perhaps compared to any siblings you may have had, or which caused you difficulties. These might include social and sensory issues, meltdowns and obsessive behaviours.

During childhood did you:

- Have sensory issues (which are often worse in childhood than adulthood)

- Emotional meltdowns

- Trouble interacting with peers and adults

- Anxiety

- Repetitive behaviours

- Obsessive behaviours
- A strong desire to be alone
- Trouble adapting to change

4 HOW DO I GET A DIAGNOSIS (AND DO I NEED ONE)?

If you're currently undiagnosed, you may be at the stage where you're considering a formal diagnosis.

Some of the main reasons for pursuing a diagnosis include:

- Gaining a clear explanation for things which have happened in the past.
- Accessing resources (including therapeutic resources or support at work) which may be available to people with autism.
- Receiving the clarity and reassurance of a formal diagnosis from a recognised clinician.
- Being able to share news of your autism diagnosis with friends/ colleagues/ family so that they can become supportive in the right way.
- Overturning a previous diagnosis which may have been incorrect.

There are, therefore, several valid reasons for seeking a

psychiatric evaluation to explore whether or not you may have autism. However, many women run into difficulties because being referred for a diagnosis is not as straightforward as you might expect.

Firstly, before you even get as far as talking to your primary care giver or psychiatrist about the possibility that you might have autism, you may be feeling doubtful about whether or not you will benefit in any way from a diagnosis. If you've held down a job, fulfilled other roles including being a daughter, mother, friend and partner and you've muddled through, aren't you pretty much…ok? If you do have autism, it's pretty mild, isn't it? It's not like *real* autism, is it? This, at least, is how many friends, family, doctors and even psychiatrists may view your condition. They don't recognise the impact that autism has on you because you seem to function "ok". However, the fact that you're "high-functioning" and skilled at masking doesn't mean that you, or anyone else, should dismiss your autism as irrelevant. Although, outwardly, you might appear to cope, your autistic symptoms may still be having a significant effect on your life.

My experience is typical of so many women, certainly in the UK and any other countries where women attempt to access psychiatric evaluation as part of a freely available healthcare package. After my therapist suggested I might have autism, and following several months of intensive research during which I concluded that my symptoms fitted very closely with autism, I plucked up the courage to visit my doctor. To put this in context, I have a real hatred of visiting doctors, which goes right back to my childhood. I have to be extremely ill before I set foot in a surgery, so it took a lot of emotional energy and planning for me to visit my doctor in the first place.

I went well prepared. I printed out several tests from the internet, all of which placed me firmly in the "borderline" category for autism. I printed out an article on women's autism which had a checklist of women's symptoms, the vast majority of which I had ticked. I was prepared to explain precisely how I would benefit from a diagnosis, noting that I had previously been diagnosed with anxiety and depression and that, not only did I put a considerable amount of effort into managing these conditions, including regularly seeing private therapists, but that I would like to make sure I had an accurate diagnosis which would allow me to access the right type of therapy. I also explained that a diagnosis of autism would ensure I accessed the correct support from friends and family in managing my condition and that it would help me make sense of a very troubled childhood, an awareness of which would be therapeutically beneficial to me in the present. The doctor listened patiently and did his own quick screening test, which also confirmed I was "borderline" autistic.

Here's how the conversation proceeded:

Doctor: "Tell me about your life - work, family etc."

Me: "I work as a therapist and I train other people to be therapists. I do a lot of writing, designing courses and stuff. I have two sons – 20 and 9 – and I live with my partner and our younger son".

Doctor: "Would you say you enjoy your life?".

Me: "Well, I've worked extremely hard to create a life which I enjoy most of the time. I've experienced extreme anxiety and bouts of depression throughout my life. I can just about manage things now because I've got myself and my work organised, but I get very exhausted and overwhelmed and sometimes my anxiety is hard to cope with. I have to regularly see a counsellor just to help me manage with life".

Doctor: "So, how would a diagnosis of autism help?".

Me: "Well, for one thing, I could make sure I was accessing the right kind of therapy. There are particular approaches which can help. Instead of paying privately, I might be able to access some resources for people with autism. If I had a diagnosis it would just help me manage my whole life better, make sure I got the right support, be more accepting of myself - and it's that lack of acceptance which is always at the route of my anxiety and depression. It would help me greatly manage my day-to-day life, and especially deal with my anxiety. It would also help me make sense of my childhood, which was pretty difficult".

Doctor: "Mmmn. You don't seem like you're autistic…you seem pretty normal…".

Me: "I make a huge effort every single day to pass as normal. You should have seen how worked up I was just about coming here - I can't handle going to the doctor. Ever since I was a kid I've felt weird, and I was bullied because of it, but you learn how to appear normal. Autistic women do at any rate".

Doctor: "But you work as a therapist. Don't you need to be able to empathise for that?".

Me: "Yes, I do. People with autism often have deep empathy for other people. And I like the structured way of talking to clients. I can do that fine but put me in a party with half a dozen people and I'll probably feel like fainting at some point, I get so confused and overwhelmed".

Doctor: "Well, I'm still a bit confused about what you're going to get out of this or whether it's worthwhile pursuing a diagnosis, but I will make a referral for you to see a psychiatrist".

I came out feeling elated. I'd convinced the doctor to refer me! I suddenly felt like a huge weight had been lifted from my shoulders. This *was* what I really needed.

A few weeks later, the doctor called me. "I'm afraid the psychiatrist says you don't qualify for a diagnosis. He doesn't agree that you're on the spectrum and he cannot see how you'll benefit from a diagnosis. I have to say, I'm in agreement".

I was deeply upset (although part of me, the part which always tried to fit in, no matter how painful it was, felt complemented that I was thought of as "too normal" to be diagnosed) and decided to drop the issue for the time being. I'm not confrontational if I can possibly avoid it and I couldn't face visiting the doctor again and going through the process of trying to convince people that I was deserving of a diagnosis.

I wrestled with the decision about whether or not to pursue a private diagnosis for some time. On the one hand, I had absolutely no doubt that I had autism and wasn't quite sure how a formal diagnosis could offer me much more assurance. But on the other hand, I wanted the clarity of a formal diagnosis. Eventually, I found a psychiatrist and went through the psychiatric diagnosis over zoom. It was very straightforward and took about two hours. I had to fill in several forms before hand, detailing memories about childhood and how I experienced the world and, during the psychiatric interview, I was asked a series of questions, some of which were open ended enough to allow me to go into considerable detail. At the end of the assessment, the psychiatrist confirmed what I was already pretty sure about - that I had autism. She did, however, also stress the effect that childhood trauma had had on me and the importance of considering this during therapy.

For me, the process was straightforward and, I think because there had been such a long lead in time, there were no particular surprises. I had already come to terms with the fact that I had autism and had started to adjust my life accordingly. Whilst the diagnosis didn't change anything, particularly, I felt more comfortable having a formal diagnosis.

Research into the experience of late-diagnosed women shows that most women find that diagnosis positively impacts their life. In contrast to undiagnosed women, who often feel different, misunderstood or lonely, and who tend to explain their social difficulties as the result of personality traits[55], late diagnosed women feel an increased sense of confidence and ability to express their opinions[56]. Some women experience a greater sense of belonging and accepting following diagnosis[57], in addition to greater self-compassion and sense of agency[58]. Post-diagnosis, some women see themselves as potential mentors for other women[59] or regard themselves as experts on autism[60].

Not everyone experiences the positive effects of a diagnosis instantaneously, however. The tendency towards later diagnosis[61] and the diagnostic process can be extremely difficult for some women[62]. Being labelled as "not normal" can be hard to deal with[63]. Satisfaction with the diagnostic process is often linked to the extent of delays, the number of professionals seen, the quality of information given at diagnosis and levels of post-diagnostic support[64].

Here are some issues which you might face when pursuing a diagnosis.

Keep fighting (and access support)

Following the setback from my GP, I decided to leave matters until I came to the decision to pay for a private diagnosis. I was busy with my business and didn't want the emotional upheaval and effort that pursuing a diagnosis would have taken me. I know myself well enough to know that it would have required all my attention and I needed to focus on earning a living. If a diagnosis is important to you, and you are better equipped emotionally than I was in pursuing one, then please make sure you remember that you have a right to be diagnosed. You're as deserving of a diagnosis as anyone else is. There may be charities or other organisations who can support you in your efforts. Many women need to push several times before being referred and are regularly fobbed off with the "you're too normal/ you can smile/ you can make eye contact" line.

Not all psychiatrists are aware of the how women experience ASD

Awareness of women and autism is growing, but it's still a comparatively recent field. If you are being referred to a psychiatrist through a free healthcare system or via your health insurance, you won't have much say (if any) over your choice of psychiatrist. Unless the psychiatrist who you are referred to is well aware of the ways in which autism affects women, it is possible that you will not receive a diagnosis of autism on the basis that you don't fit the more narrowly defined "male" criteria.

Be well prepared

At all stages, prepare as much as you can, from taking along evidence of diagnostic tests to articles about women with autism. As part of your diagnosis, the practitioner will often want to talk to your parent about how you acted as a child. If your parent is still alive but is unable to attend a discussion, you can ask them questions about yourself as a child, asking them to describe how you interacted with them and your siblings, as well as other children and adults. You can ask them to recall what they remember about any sensory issues you might have had (around things like noise, clothes, food and touch) and about repetitive and rigid behaviours, in addition to emotional regulation. Gain as much information as you can if your parents are alive for use during the diagnostic process.

Consider going private

If you are in a position where you are able to pay for a diagnosis, you will be able to exercise more control over your choice of psychiatrist and choose someone who specialises in working with women with autism. Another advantage of a private diagnosis is that it can cut the waiting times down considerably. The big drawback is the financial outlay. In the UK, you can expect to pay between about £1500 and £2000 GBP which is enough to put it beyond the reach of many people, unfortunately.

What happens during a psychiatric diagnosis?

The practitioner will ask you detailed questions about your childhood and current life. You can expect the whole process to take a few hours. You may be asked to fill out questionnaires in advance, relating to issues such as career, education, family, friends, interests, relationships, emotional regulation, sensory experiences and your childhood. The practitioner may well want to talk to your parent or, at least, to have access to a written review by your parent. The level of detail the practitioner will go into will be far more in depth than any diagnostic testing available on the internet and will include questions of a more "open" nature to allow you to go into detail about your experience. You will be asked to attend one or more appointments and there may be one or more people present during your assessment (although you may often be seen by a single psychiatrist). Appointments may vary from an hour and a half to several hours (with breaks) and some women find it traumatic going into detail about their lives. Many women find it a very cathartic experience, though, and worth the effort when they do receive their diagnosis. It is important to remember that pursuing a formal diagnosis also opens up the possibility of an alternative diagnosis. Some of the symptoms evident in women with autism may be similar to symptoms of a personality disorder or other psychiatric condition and pursuing a diagnosis involves being open to a range of possibilities other than autism.

Whether or not you go through the process of a formal diagnosis is a decision which only you can make. There is such diversity of experience between women who are referred for a diagnosis that it is impossible to say exactly what your experience will be.

Describing her experience of diagnosis, Tonya told me, "It was horrible. I nearly vomited beforehand. I don't like talking about myself. Anyway, there were two people on the panel – a psychiatrist and an assistant, I think. They just bluntly went through this huge list of questions. It took hours. I didn't feel that listened to, but they did diagnose me at the end".

Conversely, Alison described a very different process in which she felt she and her psychiatrist were working in close collaboration. "He asked loads of open questions and I actually enjoyed having the chance to talk about my childhood. He asked me whether I thought I had autism and I told him I did, based on what I'd read about it. Then at the end of our meeting – which was about two hours – he sort of smiled when he gave me his opinion. That I had autism".

Like me, some women have a negative response very early on in their journey which can put them off pursuing a formal diagnosis.

"I went to my GP and, having read some advice on the internet, felt I was very well prepared. I took along a test and my score. I explained my reasons for wanting a diagnosis and why I felt I had autism. He told me to go away and think about it because he couldn't see that I had autism and he didn't know a diagnosis would help me. I hate confrontation and it was such a big deal for me to visit him in the first place that I just didn't go back", Joni told me.

Melanie told me that, "I was diagnosed with Bipolar Disorder years ago. Then they thought I had ADHD. When I started reading about autism, I thought, 'I think this is what I've got!'. So I went back and the psychiatrist didn't want to see me again. I gave up".

Jo did see a psychiatrist and, despite the research she had conducted into women with autism and the evidence she took along to support her argument, she described the diagnostic process she experienced as being, "More appropriate to a 12 year old boy. It didn't seem to have much relevance to me as a middle aged woman. It didn't match with what I'd read about women's experiences. I came out of it without a diagnosis of autism. I visited a different psychiatrist two years later who specialised in working with women with autism and received a diagnosis".

Some women choose to self-diagnose in contrast to going through the sometimes difficult and expensive process of a psychiatric diagnosis.

Jenny said she was content to self-diagnose because, "I just don't want to go through the whole process of a full diagnosis. Even if I can access it for free, I don't like doctors. I'm concerned my autism could be missed. I've read so much now I'm pretty convinced I'm on the spectrum, so I'll just stick with that".

Billie explained that, although she could see the benefits of a psychiatric diagnosis, "I do believe I have autism, from the research I've done, but I think I'm at the very mild end of the spectrum. It's been helpful for me to say 'yes, there's a reason I am the way I am' and I'm ok at stopping with that self-realisation. I don't feel I need a full diagnosis to tell me what I already know".

Val told me, "I'm not going to pursue a diagnosis. I can see how it would have been useful when I was younger, but I'm not sure how I'll benefit from it now. I have the confidence to say I'm pretty sure I have autism and that I'll continue to create my life in a way which is right for me. That's a journey I've already started and I don't think a label, at this stage in my life, is going to make much difference".

Pursuing a formal diagnosis is, if possible, desirable given the fact that autism symptoms may present similarly to trauma related, or other psychiatric, symptoms. Many women initially explore autism because of the social difficulties and emotional regulation issues they have experienced. They may also wonder whether they have autism because they have a history of mental health issues including anxiety and depression and problems in coping with day-to-day life. Even if it turns out that you don't have autism, during the diagnostic process, you will receive other useful information about the issues which affect you. Self-diagnosis does run the risk of incorrect diagnosis, which could mean that you're not accessing the right type of support.

For instance, if you're at the start of your journey, how do you know whether your social symptoms are due to autism or whether they are the result of childhood trauma? When it comes to social interaction, being raised in an abusive environment, whether the abuse was emotional, physical or sexual, could have resulted in issues with social interaction well before you reached your teenage years. Whilst autism could explain why you feel different, isolated or weird, so could the fact that you grew up with an emotionally abusive parent who instilled in you that you were defective in some way. No matter how subtle the emotional abuse is, if you're criticised, emotionally deprived and made to feel that you're less than perfect just as you are, you'll carry that awareness into all your social interactions. One of the difficulties involved in addressing this question is that women with autism may be more susceptible to childhood abuse and so, by the time they've reached adulthood, in addition to autism they may also have endured years of childhood trauma.

Relying on purely social interactions or emotional regulation issues is not enough to diagnose autism. You need to ask yourself whether you have always experienced this type of difficulty with social interaction or whether it is something which appeared at some point during your childhood. Enlisting the help of friends and family who have known you since your earliest days can be useful here. Was there something which seemed to trigger a change in you during your pre-school years, for instance (such as the birth of a sibling, house move or some other potentially traumatic event)? Going back further than your teenage years, what were your interactions like with other children?

Looking beyond the social difficulties autism might cause, did you have issues with sensory processing? How intense were these difficulties? When I talk to most autistic people, they can name extreme issues with sensory processing, whether it's a dislike of loud noises or scratchy clothes. How intense are these processing issues? Are they at the forefront of your mind or have you had to search to recall them? Without intentionally trying to do so, it's quite easy to make sensory processing issues fit the profile of autism spectrum disorder because most of us have some dislikes. Other diagnostic criteria include obsessive interests, noticing patterns in things and a predilection to "what if then" thinking, which translates into trying to dig beneath the surface for an answer. How do you cope with disruption to your routines? Do you have intense special interests? In exploring whether you may have autism, it is important to explore the full range of autistic experience.

Traditionally, many women with autism have slipped through the diagnostic net because the criteria have been too strictly defined and too geared towards men. There is the possibility, however, that some women are self-identifying too quickly with a diagnosis when, in fact, there are other underlying causes for their issues.

One of the reasons that it matters whether your current issues are due to autism or childhood trauma is because it can help you seek out the appropriate help. If childhood trauma has had long lasting effects on social interaction, for instance, then therapy which focuses on the root causes of that trauma may be of help. If autism is the cause, then it may be more helpful to seek out therapy which focuses on emotional and social management techniques.

In my case, I certainly had a whole host of extreme sensory issues as a child and a complete obsession with words and spelling. I certainly displayed "what if, then" thinking from an early age and would spend ages trying to work out how things worked (my mother tells a story of how, as a toddler, I spent an inordinate amount of time opening and shutting a door to establish how the mechanism worked). I was always studious and had far reaching obsessions with pop bands. I was, and am, ridiculously sensitive to noise and sensations. I couldn't touch grapes or bananas due to the feel of their skin. I couldn't have my hair tied back. I developed OCD behaviours (which are often misdiagnosed or exist as a comorbidity with ASD) around doors having to be closed, counting, hand washing and rituals. I've always had issues with social situations and found it almost impossible to make eye contact. But I also grew up in a highly dysfunctional family where life was extremely stressful. My own theory is that I responded to the complex emotional environment in which I was raised in the way I did because I was autistic. I also suspect that, had I been born into a less chaotic and emotionally demanding family, I wouldn't have gone onto develop the extreme issues I did.

Whilst autism may provide an explanation for your symptoms, pursuing a formal diagnosis will help establish, with the help of an expert, whether there is a different underlying cause for your symptoms which may present similarly to autism.

Exercise

Take some time to do the following exercise. Keep a note of your responses so that you can refer to them in the future when you need to reiterate the potential benefits of diagnosis and the difficulties you may encounter.

In what ways will a diagnosis of autism help you towards your journey of authenticity?

What emotions do you expect to arise, or what emotions have you experienced, as a result of your autism diagnosis?

5 I HAVE AUTISM! SO, WHAT NOW?

Whether you have chosen to self-diagnose, or you have received a diagnosis from a qualified professional, the big question is, "what next?". How do you take this awareness, and your identification as having autism, forwards?

Understanding that your brain works in a particular way is a momentous step on your journey towards self-discovery and, like anything else important in life, it stirs up all kinds of emotions. No matter how excited you feel about the impact your autism diagnosis might have on you, it's likely that you'll experience a wide range of other emotions; some of which are easier to deal with than others.

It is important, during the earlier stages, to be patient with yourself and to be aware that there are no "good" and "bad" emotional responses. Whatever you're feeling is understandable, and it will shift and change as you continue on your journey. If you've experienced difficulties throughout your life due to undiagnosed autism, it's understandable if you feel angry and frustrated when you finally discover the root cause of those difficulties. If you've been singled out and bullied due to your differences, it's possible that you might experience shame when those differences are given a label. And, one day, you might just wake up and breathe a huge sigh of relief that you have a diagnosis which can help you live life in a more authentic way.

The way you respond to, and deal with, your diagnosis will be unique to you, but here are some of the emotions that many women experience.

Fear

No matter how hard your life journey may have been so far, muddling through and trying to cope might seem like a better option than admitting that, because of the way your brain works, some things will always require more effort for you than they do for other people. Once you've received a diagnosis you may feel very scared. How are you going to live a normal life with autism?

Maureen felt extremely upset post-diagnosis. "I wish I could see this as a positive but I'm just thinking, how am I going to live the life I want to live? Can I keep working in retail when I find things this hard? Can I even think of having a normal life? I'm just feeling anxious about the future at the moment".

Sandy told me, "I'm really scared just now. I don't know how I'm supposed to live as someone with autism. Part of me feels I was better off not knowing. I've managed so far. I'm scared about telling other people and I'm scared about having a 'condition'".

Tonya described feeling overwhelmed. "I don't know what to make of it yet. I have good days and bad days. I'm worried now that it's been given a name. More worried than I did just sort of wondering if there was something which explained the way I was".

I initially felt some fear, too. I'd got so used to living life a certain way and, although it might have been very tough at times, I'd managed. I was worried about taking on a "label", somehow making the (irrational) connection that having a diagnosis would make life even harder. How was I going to cope with everything I had to deal with in life as a woman with autism spectrum disorder? My reasoning wasn't particularly rational, as I'd *always* coped with life as a woman with autism. I just didn't know it.

Being fearful is completely understandable. This is a big deal. With any type of psychiatric diagnosis, there is always a feeling of trepidation. Changing things, including accepting that there is a reason for the way we act and the lives we have lived so far, is a scary proposition. In a future chapter, we will look at how you can begin to reframe your fearful response as a starting point to explore where the fear stems from and what questions might need genuinely addressing. Receiving a diagnosis of autism can make you feel extremely vulnerable. It involves naming and revealing something about yourself which you may have taken great pains to keep hidden. Owning up to our vulnerabilities is, indeed, scary. It also provides the chance to begin to accept ourselves as we are, and to allow others to accept our true selves.

Relief

One of the biggest responses that people have to a diagnosis of autism is relief. When you understand that there's a reason for the way you act, think, and deal with life, it takes a huge amount of pressure and self-judgement off your shoulders.

For Alison, her diagnosis helped her to feel validated, which led to a sense of self-acceptance. "I always knew that some things were just very difficult for me but people always called me demanding or hyper-sensitive. That made me feel bad about myself, so I'd keep doing what was expected of me even though it could make me quite ill. When I got my diagnosis, I just felt this huge sense of relief. It's like I felt vindicated. I'm not just a super-demanding person! These things I need to do in life are really important to me and there's a reason for that".

Jo told me, "I just let out this huge sigh of relief. I felt pretty overwhelmed, almost near tears. It all made so much sense to me. My whole life".

Jada describes a feeling of elation when her psychiatrist gave her his diagnosis. "I was so happy! It was about two years from starting to think I might have autism to being diagnosed, and a bit of a battle to get the diagnosis. When he gave me his opinion, I was delighted. I could finally make sense of my past and start looking towards a different type of future".

Relief was certainly one of the emotions I experienced following my diagnosis. Up until that point, I had felt like my whole life was this extended battle. Yes, there were aspects of my life which I loved and derived a huge amount of satisfaction from, including my children, my partner, my career...but so many things were just very tough. Everyday things, in particular, caused me huge problems and I just couldn't work out why. Realising that my brain worked in a particular way due to autism started to relieve the negative feelings and the low self-esteem I had suffered from for my entire life.

There's also relief in knowing that you're not the only person out there who finds certain things difficult. There are plenty of others who, like you, may have found ways of very effectively disguising their difficulties in life. It was extremely comforting to discover a whole community of women with autism through their writings and I'd spend hours reading books and looking up research and articles on the internet. I could identify with these women who were like me in so many ways. I chose not to attend any groups, simply because I really don't feel comfortable in group settings, but it was nice to know that there was an extended physical community out there if I wanted to access it.

Maureen similarly derived comfort in making contact with other women with autism and reading about their experiences. "It feels so good to me to know that there are women out there who have had the same kind of struggles in life. They're women with jobs, families, whatever but it's been hard for them and it feels good to know there's a reason for me being the way I am and that I'm not alone".

Shame

Shame is a strong word for a strong emotion and sometimes when people receive an autism diagnosis, they feel ashamed and even disgusted with themselves, partly due to their lack of awareness about what autism is and the huge diversity of experience with autism. Especially if you've grown up being called "weird" and feeling "odd" compared to others, having a label of autism can feel like a confirmation of your weirdness.

Whatever end of the spectrum you or anyone else is on, there's nothing shameful in it. All it means is that your brain works in a particular way. It's not any worse or better than anyone else's, it's just a slightly different operating system to what the majority of people have. We need to start celebrating neurodiversity in all its shapes and colours.

Sandy expressed her shame as, "a feeling that I really was weird, odd, different, that I shouldn't be allowed out in the normal world. I felt that everyone who had bullied me for being different was justified in their actions".

Heather told me, "I'm a very liberal person. I work in mental health and support people with mental health issues. I like to think I'm very accepting and if someone else had told me they were diagnosed with autism, I'd have been interested and very supportive. But when it came to myself, I felt sort of ashamed and very judgemental. I felt like finally we all knew there was something 'wrong' with me and I wanted to keep it secret".

"I was ashamed and embarrassed. I didn't want anyone to know, especially my family. I didn't want them to think there was something wrong with me, or to feel sorry for me or talk about how they'd always known I was weird behind my back. Although I'd pursued a diagnosis, I was a bit horrified when the psychiatrist actually confirmed I had autism", Leslie told me.

Other clients have similarly felt conflicted in the shame they feel towards themselves whilst expressing an openness to the experience of others. It's important to remember that, if you feel a sense of shame at being diagnosed with autism, it doesn't mean that your values have been upturned and you're suddenly a judgemental person who vilifies people for being different. You could be the most liberal, accepting person in the world, but when it comes to your own self-judgement, you're experiencing that from the perspective of someone who may always have carried around feelings of shame and who may be operating from a point of low self-esteem. This is perfectly understandable, especially if you were made fun of for being "weird" or "different" at points in your life. If that was your experience, from your own internal perspective, having a label of autism or anything else which identifies you as differing from the "norm" has the potential to make you feel bad about yourself. Accepting that these feelings are a perfectly normal part of your journey is the first step in moving towards self-acceptance.

Regret about the past

Receiving a diagnosis of autism by the time you have reached adulthood has the capacity to bring up strong feelings of regret about your past. You may think, "if only I'd been diagnosed as a child! My life would have been so much easier!". In many ways, that's probably true. If you had been diagnosed, you could have received the support you needed whilst you were growing up. You could also have avoided, at least to some extent, the years of trying to change yourself in order to fit into a neurotypical society. A diagnosis could have helped you be more accepting of yourself from an early age and would have helped you make choices which were more true and authentic to the person you were.

You may find yourself looking back on your childhood and re-evaluating it, feeling extremely sorry for that young girl who got confused and tongue-tied, who didn't understand the playground rules and who tried so hard to do what others expected that she ignored her own passions and interests. You may feel a sense of regret about personal and professional choices you took throughout your life because, if you had known you had autism, it would have helped you make more informed choices.

Unfortunately, hindsight is the one thing that none of us have access to and it's important is to let go of any blame of yourself for being unaware that you had particular needs. There is, simply, nothing you can do to change what has happened in the past. You may feel that your parents could have done more to get you the help you needed, but depending on what era you grew up in, there was very little awareness and perhaps very little access to the right resources. I was a child in the 1970s and, although I displayed a whole range of problematic behaviours, my parents never sought out any help for me. In the UK at that time, therapy simply wasn't a consideration and despite *my* many problems, I was quite an "unproblematic" child. I generally did what I was told, stayed quiet and invisible, and my difficulties surfaced as migraines and binge eating. I suspect, though, that even if my parents had sought out help for me, I may well not have received a diagnosis of autism at that point in time, given the lack of awareness of how girls display symptoms.

Maureen, who was recently diagnosed in her forties when she came to see me, expressed deep regret with regard to her earlier experiences, "I just wish I had known sooner. I wouldn't have wasted so much time and energy into trying to be like everyone else. I could have been happier being me".

Jada also felt regret that, "I did what was expected of me. I had children far too young. There was this pressure within my family to have kids, but I had this brain that loved doing stuff, puzzles, painting, and I just ignored the stuff that made me feel whole".

Rosa felt that, had she known she had autism, she would have been much kinder to herself growing up. "I hated that I felt different to other girls but the more I hated it, the more effort I put into trying to be the same as them. I wish I could go back and just be more honest about who I was".

Regret is a perfectly understandable response but it's important to remember that all of your experiences, good and bad, have contributed to the person you are today. The tenacity, determination, strength and ability to come up with solutions to life's difficulties are all qualities which will have been strengthened in you as you have dealt with your experiences throughout your life.

Acceptance

Somewhere down the line, when you've come to terms with any of the negative responses which may accompany a diagnosis of autism, you might find yourself moving to a point not only of accepting but of actually embracing your diagnosis. Having autism and being unaware of it can cause you a lot of problems, but once you have that awareness it means you can begin looking at the world through different eyes; from the perspective of someone who has particular needs and whose experience to date has been shaped by those needs. Instead of putting yourself down, you may notice how well you have done to cope. Instead of criticizing yourself, discovering you have autism can help you to accept your uniqueness and individuality. Accepting that your brain works in a particular way and that there's absolutely nothing wrong in that is a huge step towards accepting yourself more generally and becoming compassionate towards yourself.

You can also recognise that you have skills and abilities in particular areas. You may see things that other people don't and have a unique sense of humour or creative streak; your autistic mind will, undoubtedly, have given you a valuable take on the world around you. Once you realise your brain works in a certain way, you can begin to respect what you need to make you happy. Some of those activities, experiences and ways of being will bring great joy into your life and have the potential to make the world a better place, too.

Tonya told me, "I had always been 'bookish', all the way through school. Then I went to university, and finally ended up working as an academic. I then got married, had two kids and although I kept working, I did what so many women do and went part time, did all the house work and most of the childcare. I love my kids but I hate the domestic stuff…I missed being able to focus all day on research…I felt like I was a terrible mother but since my diagnosis, I've gone full time at work again. I've recognised that I need that intense research work in my life to be happy and I've let go of the guilt around parenting".

Amy described how she'd downplayed what she saw as her differences. "I always felt I had this amazing affinity with animals but as a teenager I tried to ignore it, went down a different route and went into a different career. I know realise I really do have a special thing with animals and I'm determined to work with them in some capacity".

For Rosa, the eventual acceptance of her autism meant accepting herself as a whole person. "I'd never liked myself much. I didn't like that I had anxiety, that I found things difficult socially, that I was a quiet, introverted kid and an awkward adult. When I was diagnosed with autism, I began to like myself for who I was. It didn't happen overnight, but it did happen".

Self-acceptance, or embracement, doesn't happen overnight and recognising and respecting where you are on your personal journey is important.

Billie told me, "I sometimes read about women with autism saying how wonderful it is that they're autistic. Being sort of loud and proud. I don't think it's wonderful and I'm not sure I ever will. Autism makes my life very hard. But I am working on, at least, accepting that I have autism and that doesn't make me a bad person. That's a starting point, I guess".

Struggling with a diagnosis of ASD

It's perfectly normal to struggle with a diagnosis of autism. It's important to take time to come to terms with it and to realise that, like any transitional stage, with self-patience and kindness you will be able to lead a more authentic life as a result of your diagnosis. Having a label of autism doesn't make you any different to who you were the day, week or year before. And it doesn't define you, either. You may have autism but you're also the sum part of every experience you've ever had in life. As with any condition, *you have* autism; it doesn't have you. You're a complex, multi-faceted person who has the opportunity to use your diagnosis as a time of potential and growth as you choose to move forwards in life from a point of awareness.

Exercise:

Take a few minutes to note down any emotions which come up for you when you think about the fact that you have autism. Perhaps you will identify with the emotional responses listed above or perhaps you will have responded in a different way.

Once you have written down your emotions, take some time to explore what is underlying those emotions. For instance, if you have written down "fear" – take a note of what you are fearful about. This can become your starting point for addressing your fear.

6 IMAGINING AN AUTHENTIC LIFE

Learning what your diagnosis of ASD means to you takes time. There'll be days when you feel great about it, days when you question whether you have been correctly diagnosed (by yourself or a professional) and days when you want to shake off the diagnosis altogether. "Coming to terms" with something as big as a diagnosis of autism doesn't happen overnight but as you begin to experiment with how it feels to be a woman with autism you can ask yourself, "how will this knowledge help me lead the life I want and deserve?".

An inherent desire to lead an authentic life is evident from the answer that so many of my clients offer when I ask them how they imagine their lives might change as a result of their autism diagnosis. Again and again, the reply is, "I want to feel more authentic". As an adult woman, if you have traversed your life so far with undiagnosed autism, you may well have learned how to act in ways which other people find acceptable, to adapt and ignore your own needs and desires to appear normal and to push aside what really makes you tick (if what makes you tick makes other people uncomfortable). Acting this way means you can go through life relatively unnoticed, which is a blessed relief if you were subjected to bullying or mockery as a result of your differences. Women with autism become experts at camouflaging themselves in order to fit in, but the cost of this strategy is that you become so good at changing your colours whenever you need to that you don't really know what your true colours are.

Camouflaging behaviours include forcing yourself to make eye contact, using memory techniques to remember suitable conversation topics, suppressing autistic tendencies and/ or trying to engage in "normal" social behaviours[65]. This can include making an effort not to talk too much about a topic you're interested in or practicing looking at a partner's facial expression before you respond[66], filling pauses in conversation[67] and using gestures[68], all of which can help with everything from making friends to performing well during a job interview[69]. Women view camouflaging as a means to make social connections and maintain friendships[70], and some women report using masking in order to avoid physical, emotional or verbal abuse[71]. Many learn to camouflage from such an early age that it becomes their "natural" behaviour, rather than a conscious choice[72]. Autistic women aren't the only people to camouflage, but they are more likely to camouflage than neurotypicals or autistic men[73,74,75] and even between autistic men and women who camouflage, women appear to use different camouflaging techniques to men[76].

You might ask, if you've managed to get by reasonably ok by being all things to all people, what is the point in becoming the "true you"? Aren't you just risking inviting criticism and judgement? Rejection and ridicule? Potentially, all those things you've tried so hard to avoid?

The fact is, you may well have survived by masking who you really are, and it's certainly an understandable coping mechanism, particularly when you're a child and younger adult and are less empowered in terms of decision making and creating your own social circle. But do you want to continue leading a life where you mask who you really are? Or do you want to pursue a life where you put your own needs and wants centre stage and start paying attention to what makes you happy and fulfilled? Do you deserve to live a life which is just ok? Or do you deserve something better?

At the start of their journey, although many women with autism don't yet know what an authentic life might be, they have an underlying feeling that they're not being true to themselves in their current guise.

For me, the discovery that I had ASD has had a profound impact on how I live my life. In some ways, the impact is greatest in the mundane, day-to-day stuff which much of our lives are made up of. I have realised that it is extremely difficult for me to take on too many responsibilities which take me away from the interests and passions which make me thrive, namely writing and conducting research. I love getting completely absorbed in my work and react very adversely when I have too many interruptions. After realising just how badly these types of disruptions affected me, I made far more of an effort to say "no" when I had to. It wasn't easy, but my diagnosis of autism helped me realise just how crucial it was to my mental and physical health to stop saying "yes" to everyone's demands, especially when those demands threw me off course with regards to work.

When I received my diagnosis, I realised I had to find a way of pursuing what I really loved. It gave me the courage to turn away work which didn't make my heart sing and to spend more time on what I cared about, even when it wasn't bringing in money. Before my diagnosis, I had an underlying belief that it was self-indulgent to follow my passions. Post-diagnosis, I knew pursuing my interests was vital to my mental and physical health. I gained clarity about what my brain *needed* in terms of creative and intellectual stimulation. And I put in more effort to meet those needs.

Another huge impact of my diagnosis was in terms of choosing the types of social activities which felt right for me, and turning down those which I didn't want to be involved in. Prior to this, I used to feel bad about not enjoying myself when I was out. I felt I should turn up to things, even though I knew they would leave me completely shattered afterwards. I felt guilty about making elaborate excuses or having "get out clauses" built into any social event I was forced to attend. Alcohol had always been my way of coping with such situations but since I'd massively reduced my alcohol intake, the social situations just seemed more unbearable and I felt increasingly conflicted. I liked people on a one-to-one basis where I could have interesting discussions with them, I just didn't like being in groups, particularly where the discussions were of a "small talk" nature. There are times when I've been accused of being stand-offish, pretentious and unfriendly in social groups but what might come across as stand-offishness to other people is actually me making a huge effort to be sociable. Nobody sees the internal effort I'm putting into making conversation and trying to keep track of what has been said while my mind goes blank or is searching desperately through its list of appropriate responses. I don't choose to be like that. I just am. And I've accepted that.

I found it far easier, after my diagnosis, to be honest with myself, which included recognising and respecting that I have a strong need to spend time on my own. I have two children and a partner, all of whom I love and enjoy spending time with, but I also crave my own company. If I don't get that time alone, I become agitated and bad tempered. Post-diagnosis, if I knew that going to a family "do" would mean I'd miss out on time alone before a busy work week, I learned to prioritise that necessary time on my own.

Many of these adaptations aren't earth shattering in their

own right, but it's incredible how they have added up to completely change my life. Being honest about what you need to do to take care of yourself and fulfil your needs is crucial in terms of leading an authentic life.

Another reason to consider moving beyond camouflaging, is due to the impact it can have on your mental health. Research has shown that women who attempt to camouflage their autistic traits tend to experience low self-esteem, stress, exhaustion, anxiety and depression[77,78] and may have difficulties struggling in everyday life and experience suicidal thoughts[79]. Although autistic men also describe camouflaging behaviours[80], because women make more of an effort to "fit in" socially through masking their autism than men do, they tend to experience more severe mental health issues than men[81-83], and even "mild" autism has been linked with an increased risk of mental illness[84-86]. The link between autism and a range of mental health concerns isn't to say that all mental health issues in women are a direct result of autism, as some autistic women may experience mental health issues for other reasons[87,88].

Why does camouflaging cause women so many problems? On a logical level, it seems to make sense to adopt behaviours which allow you to fit in and pass in a neurotypical world. On the other hand, we know there is a link between camouflaging and psychological distress, even after accounting for the severity of autistic traits[89]. It's not entirely clear whether the link between camouflaging behaviours and mental health issues is related to the underlying reasons which cause women to camouflage, including low self-esteem, low self-acceptance and social isolation, or whether they develop mental health issues *because* they adopt camouflaging behaviours[90]. What we do know is that women's experiences of camouflaging are predominantly negative[91].

Camouflaging also involves downplaying one's own feelings of distress, as revealed in one study where girls masked their own feelings of unhappiness and anxiety in social situations in order to prevent their relationships from breaking down[92]. I became so adept at masking my own upset and distress, which was considerable, from childhood onwards that people didn't know there was anything wrong with me. In secret, I would drink salt water to try and make myself sick so that I didn't have to go to school. I would rub my legs on the pebble-dashed garage wall, until they were raw, which provided me with a sense of relief. And, on several occasions, I would sit at the kitchen table with a carving knife held above my wrist, contemplating how it would feel to end it all. Part of my ability to mask my feelings was as the result of growing up in a family where it was considered indulgent to express any "negative" emotions. Part of it was due to the immensity of the emotions which I experienced and which I could not deal with.

My masking skills often backfired for me, for instance when I suffered extreme anxiety during my final year at university. There were whole days when my anxiety was so bad that I couldn't breathe properly. But I always had a smile on my face, always turned up and handed work in one time. Nobody knew about my anxiety or about the fact that I drank heavily every day to self-medicate. Another girl in my class also experienced extreme anxiety during her final year. Unlike me, she had been open about her mental health issues and had sought support and medication. She had people's understanding and empathy and support from the university. I wanted to scream out loud that I'd had a nightmare couple of years, that I'd cut off my hair in a mad moment, that every day was a struggle and that my anxiety was so bad I could barely function. But it was too late. I'd fooled everyone into thinking I was ok.

Masking, therefore, goes beyond simply watching what words you use or making sure you don't talk about your favourite subject for too long. It involves camouflaging your emotional responses to such an extent that you can appear devoid of emotion to others. To consistently be in such pain and to cover it up so effectively means that it is difficult to ask for help or for others to recognise that you are in need of support.

It's easy to mistakenly think that women who have average or higher than average levels of intellectual functioning have an easier time functioning in their daily lives than women with a lower level of intellectual functioning. However many high-functioning women have difficulties securing or maintaining full time employment and rely heavily on support from family[93,94].

Despite appearing to cope with life, many adult women experience a significant amount of distress[95]. When it comes to the link between autism and mental health, research has shown that the relationship between camouflaging efforts and mental health is linked to the *degree of camouflaging behaviours* rather than the severity of the autistic traits which are being masked[96]. Similarly, suicidality has been linked to camouflaging behaviours as opposed to the severity of autistic traits in both women and men[97].

Josie described herself as, "desperate to talk about things which interest me, and go on and on about them. If something sparks my interest, I want to jump in. I've really had to learn how to hold myself back but I've got to the point I worry about everything I might say or do and don't feel like I'm being myself at all when I'm in a group".

Jo said that she, "felt a loss of identity. I'm so skilled at masking and passing as normal that I started to lose sight of who I am and what I like. At one time, I felt like taking my own life".

Alison described a similar experience and noted, "It's not just that I mask around other people, which I do. But it's almost like I camouflage all the time. I started agreeing with others that my interests were a bit odd. That I was a bit odd. And I don't even know who I am when I'm on my own now".

Working towards authenticity

Whilst women often express a desire to lead a more authentic life, they have difficulty in imagining and articulating what this authentic life might be. When you've become adept at fitting in and ignoring your needs, it can be difficult to work out what you really need and want from life. The starting point for many women is simply realising that something has to change. That the life they're living doesn't feel true or supportive or authentic. Having awareness that something *isn't* authentic is a starting point for exploring what authenticity might be.

When exploring what your authentic life might look and feel like, you can consider the following.

Congruence between, values, beliefs and actions

"Being authentic" is hard to define. It's one of those phrases which we all know and yet…what does it actually mean? We all have things that, deep down, we care about. These might include work, hobbies, time on our own, family, friends, animals, music, art and causes we are passionate about. Being authentic means being able to attend to the things in your life which really matter to you. It means being able to identify what you need and want from life and work on pursuing those needs and wants. It means tapping into that sense of *you* when you feel a sense of satisfaction and fulfilment, and it means taking decisions and actions which allow you to pursue this experience of satisfaction and fulfilment. Once you have made contact with your true self, being authentic means having the confidence to speak up for what you believe in and allow yourself to be seen for who you are. Perhaps your life has felt more authentic to you at some points than it currently does. What was it about this previous point in life which felt authentic?

We often talk about authenticity in terms of pursuing our values. What exactly do we mean by values? Values are those things that are important to you in the way you think and act. When we're inauthentic, we might act in a way which serves other people's values even when our choices don't reflect what matters to us. When you have autism, you may have internalised the message early on that what matters to you is weird or insignificant. When you and others around you have called into question your values from an early age, it can be difficult to work out exactly what your values are. But no matter how much you've been pulled about over the years or criticised for thinking, feeling and acting in particular ways, you can now get in touch with what you care about in life.

Values can be deep and meaningful and projected towards the good of others – and include things like being honest, caring for animals and the environment, and being loving and kind – but they also involve taking care of yourself. For instance, your values could include time for having fun, pursuing interests and self-care. Your values could include creating healthy emotional boundaries for yourself and creating safe spaces. *Your* values are what matters to *you*; there's no right or wrong here.

Exercise:

What activities do you need to do in life to feel fully alive?

What do you need to do in terms of self-care to truly value yourself?

What really matters to you in terms of values?

Your authentic life is unique to you

Authenticity comes in all shapes and sizes. "Being authentic" doesn't mean living off grid, eating home-grown plants and making your own shoes. But it might do. It could equally mean working as a cut-throat lawyer, painting pictures, taking some time out of life to heal or climbing mountains in your spare time. Exploring your authenticity may involve a deep spiritual awakening or it may involve conducting rigorous scientific research. For you, authenticity might mean saying no to people and cutting down social engagements. For someone else, it might mean pursuing more meaningful social connections. The components which make up what becomes an authentic life are unique to you and your concept of authenticity will be very different to someone else's.

Committing to authenticity

On your journey towards a more authentic life, aspects of your life will need to change. Creating this change isn't easy. You'll need to learn new ways of being and acting. You might have to crawl out of a rut which, whilst limiting, might also be very comfortable. You may hurt people along the way as you take new decisions and act in different ways within relationships. It's often easier to live inauthentically than to go through this process and becoming authentic requires a high degree of commitment. You need to remind yourself that this process is worthwhile and that an authentic life has the potential to be so much more fulfilling than the life which you have led to date.

Getting acquainted with the "backstage" you

Erving Goffman used the metaphor of the theatre to describe how our lives are played out in terms of different "roles"[98]. We act, dress and communicate in particular ways in relation to other "actors", or people. As a result, we have several selves which might include being a professional, a daughter, an employee, a mother, a student and a spiritual being. Our professional self isn't going to lounge around in pyjamas and swear in meetings – but she might do so when she's with her partner. There are times, of course, when we're not on the "stage" – those times when we're on our own or with someone close to us with whom we're comfortable enough to just be "ourselves". What does this backstage version of you feel like? What does she like? What is missing from her life?

If the authentic *you* is this "backstage" version, when you're no longer playing a part, is it possible for you to bring aspects of that version of you into the forefront? To bring her into your interactions with other people? This isn't something to be undertaken overnight and it's not something to be undertaken lightly. You're in charge here. There's no pressure to reveal anything about yourself unless you feel safe and comfortable in doing so. But instead of consistently hiding your backstage self, is it possible to identify which of her qualities you *would* like to share with other people? Do you want to bring some fun into your professional role? Do you want to display your more introverted side when you're in company, without feeling the need to act in an overtly fake, confident manner? Does it feel safe to reveal some of your vulnerabilities within your close relationships? In your own personal pursuit of authenticity, is it possible for you to reveal aspects of your more authentic self to those people around you?

An authentic life feels "right"

When you are being authentic, you just feel "right". What is right depends on the situation. Feeling authentic in a professional capacity might include feeling nerves or the buzz of a deal. Feeling authentic at home might mean feeling fully relaxed and loved. It could include feeling deeply focused and engaged in a creative flow or deeply satisfied that you are making a positive impact in the world. Being authentic isn't one particular feeling or emotion as it can encompass so many feelings and emotions. It is a sense of feeling "right for you", whatever that entails and your authentic self will feel different in different situations.

Identifying the trip wires

Exploring what your authentic life might look and feel like, and a commitment to leading an authentic life is the starting point, but if you think of this as a journey, you need to be aware of the tripwires you might come across. However strong your motivation to create change, you have spent a lifetime adapting yourself to fit in with other people's expectations. No matter how strong your current commitment to becoming more authentic is, all your old beliefs about how to fit in and meet other people's needs have the potential to trip you up at any stage in your journey. You might want to do something which feels authentic, but there'll be a voice in your head telling you that you *should* be doing something else. We carry within us the voices of parents, siblings, friends and employers who can be highly critical of our attempts to pursue authenticity. You might be excited about taking a new course in flower arranging until your brother reminds you that you'll never make any money at it. Or your mum's voice will come into your head reminding you that you're shy when you experiment with new ways of communicating with your colleagues. You might be able to work out what some of the tripwires are likely to be at the start of your journey but be aware that they'll often literally come out of nowhere and stall you. When that happens, you need to take enough time to metaphorically dust yourself off and start putting one foot in front of the other again.

Exercise:

Identifying the trip wires

Name 3 beliefs which might challenge your desire to pursue an authentic life?

Identify any people in your life who will challenge your desire to pursue an authentic life.

How will you know you've been tripped up?

How will you dust yourself off and restart your journey?

Visualising an authentic future

When I work with clients in order to help them lead a more authentic life, my starting point with them is, what does *your* authentic life look like? I ask them to project into the future and describe how they feel in themselves, how they see themselves living, noting their emotions and physical experience and what their daily life involves.

Leona noticed a difference in her emotional state during this exercise, "I felt a lot calmer. What I was doing was the same as now but instead of being in a panic, I had systems in place to deal with things like work and day to day things. I cut things out of my day that I didn't want to do".

For Jada, the change was about incorporating her passions and interests into her life. "I had set up an easel in the spare room and started painting again. That felt like such a significant statement".

Josie had more time to be alone, "It just seemed like I wasn't constantly running from one thing to another. I was alone which felt nice and which rarely happens now. I had time to read a book or just be alone with my thoughts".

After clients have imagined their future, I ask them to imagine that we're meeting up again - at that point in the future which they have imagined - and ask them to tell me what they did to create the changes.

Leona told me, "I just had good systems in place, for everything from getting up and making breakfast to prioritising tasks at work. When I'm left to my own devices, I get carried away, getting so absorbed in one thing that I totally fall behind on something else. I like order, so having systems and timetables in place helped me stay calm".

Jada said she committed to taking up art again, which was a passion she had left behind due to her work and family commitments. "I reminded myself every day that this is something I love, which is important and which I *need*. I made a commitment to myself to spend some time each day at my easel even if it means ignoring the laundry or whatever".

For Josie, the change stemmed from identifying what she needed to do for herself and the damaging effects that always devoting her time to her family was having on her. "For years, I've been running after everyone all the time. It's not who I was as a child, when I'd get lost in things for hours. In my future self, I had time and I made that time by saying no to people - friends and family - by stopping feeling I had to do things just because they were expected of me. I stopped joining clubs, trying to make friends I wasn't interested in, doing things which I thought made me look normal…and I started spending more time alone which felt like it was good for my mind and was going to lead somewhere".

I invite you to do this exercise so that you can begin to clarify what your authentic life looks like, and then to work out what you need to let go of and what you need to embrace to create that life.

Exercise:

Future self

Make sure you're nice and comfortable and have at least 10 minutes.

Choose a time when you would like to be living your more authentic life (perhaps somewhere between 6 months and 2 years)

Close your eyes and imagine you have woken up at that point in the future. You are leading a more authentic life, following your ASD diagnosis.

Notice how you feel emotionally. What thoughts and feelings are you experiencing?

Notice how you feel physically. How is your wellness, fitness and strength?

Notice what you are doing. How has your day-to-day life changed? What is the same? What have you let go of or embraced?

Now, write down everything that you did to create that more authentic version of you in the future (if it helps, you can imagine you are that future version of yourself who is telling you how she achieved the changes).

As a starting point, you can consider:

What opportunities did you start saying "yes" to?

What did you start saying "no" to?

How did you nurture yourself in terms of interests, passions & alone time?

What did you do which you may have rejected as "weird" or "self-indulgent"?

7 DEVELOPING STRATEGIES

Becoming authentic isn't something which happens overnight. It takes commitment, motivation and a strategy. Hold on, you might think. Won't I just begin to experience authenticity in wonderful momentary glimpses which will eventually lead me to my authentic self? Well, whilst this type of spiritual awakening is an attractive thought, and whilst you'll certainly have some *wow* moments along the way, it's helpful to have a plan in place.

Developing strategies for dealing with situations as you pursue a more authentic life is essential. People with autism can become very easily overwhelmed by day-to-day challenges and have a tendency to focus on the small details, allowing the bigger picture to get lost in the process. Pursuing a more authentic life is a definitely "big picture" territory so if you want to avoid getting lost in the details and getting pulled in several directions, you need to have strategies in place. Many women with autism also become confused when presented with information and choice in the moment, and pre-planning can help you to avoid falling into old habits.

Jo told me that, "Sometimes people ask me a very straightforward question, or make what seems to be a straightforward request, but my initial reaction is just confusion. I say yes to things, agree on a plan…and then sometimes straight afterwards I regret it".

Pat explained, "I'm always saying I'll do things, or agreeing to stuff, without thinking about it. I actually go a bit blank when people ask me something out of the ordinary and then I make the wrong decision".

Melanie told me, "I'm fine at work or whatever. I'm ok at making decisions when I know the kinds of decisions I need to make – like, should we send this patient to this unit or the other unit. I have a strategy in place for those kinds of decisions. But when someone asks me if I want to go to a barbeque at the weekend, or whether I'm ok staying in a particular hotel, I just feel confused and overwhelmed. I'm always making the wrong choices!".

When you have autism, you might find yourself very easily thrown by requests, suggestions and choices which are presented to you unexpectedly. If something comes "out of the blue", it can be difficult to make an assessment and come up with a suitable response. Whilst you might be fine in those situations, such as in the workplace, where there is a strategy in place for particular situations, when you lack this strategy you end up signing up to all kinds of things you really don't want to.

It's very hard to stay on track with learning new ways of being with a view to becoming more authentic when you're being pulled in different directions.

One solution to this is to ensure you have strategies in place for the types of things which might come up for you as you pursue a more authentic life. Although you can't determine the *precise* situations which will make you feel confused and compromised, you know from past experience the *kinds* of situations which cause you grief afterwards when you wish you'd said "no", "I'll think about it" or "let me see and I'll get back to you".

Take some time out

Autistic people have brains which don't respond to some situations as quickly as neurotypical brains, which means that, instead of being able to respond to a request or choice with the rational, evaluating part of the brain, you go to the emotional part instead. If there isn't an exact situation which has taken place in the past, you might find it very hard to evaluate and respond appropriately.

One way of dealing with this is simply to take some time out. You may feel that if someone requests something of you or offers you a choice you need to respond immediately. In fact, you don't. You can take some time out so that you can properly evaluate the situation. If it's a pressing issue, even taking a minute or two on your own to weigh up the options can be useful. All you're doing is putting yourself on the same footing as your neurotypical counterparts. You deserve a couple of minutes to do that, don't you? If you have more time, you can take longer to consider your options before coming to a decision.

Here are some phrases which you can use to take control of the situation and create some much needed time and space.

"I know you need a decision on this, but I need to take a couple of minutes to consider it".

"That sounds interesting. Let me have a think and I'll get back to you".

"Leave that with me and I'll let you know in the morning".

Like many women with autism, you may be concerned about offending people – perhaps as the result of past occasions when you have been accused of being too blunt or honest. This sometimes results in going the other way and become so worried about seeming offensive that you bend over backwards to try and please everyone else. The above phrases are not offensive, although you will need to spend some time getting used to employing them, and they demonstrate a very reasonable request for time and space.

Change your mind

Another way in which you can deal with these types of situations which place difficult choices or requests on you is to *change your mind*. Yes, it's preferable to be straight with people initially in order to avoid causing confusion, but if you do make the wrong choice for you and it takes you half an hour/ a day/ a week to realise it...*you can change your mind*. You might find this a particularly uncomfortable thought if you have a tendency to think in terms of absolutes, or "black and white thinking", as so many people with autism do. Once you've told someone you can sit on their board of members, prepare trifle for the parents' disco or take on more overtime at work, how can you change your mind? What you've agreed to is written in stone, right? Wrong! It may cause a little disruption, or even slight annoyance, but you have the right to change your mind. And the sooner you announce your intentions, the better.

Here's an example of a situation I found myself in recently. My mother was in hospital and I booked a hotel near to the hospital in order to visit her daily. I had booked online but arrived early. The room wasn't ready and I asked if I could leave my case so I could head into town before visiting time at the hospital. The hotel owner told me, "I've got another room, a separate annexe, which is ready if you want. Perfect for the hospital, it's got a wee kitchen area so you can cook your own food". I said I'd take a look. I was shown into a separate extension, which had a single bed (instead of the double in the original room), a small kitchen area and no windows. I stood, overwhelmed by how horrible it was, how the lack of windows made it oppressive and how different it was to the lovely bright, double room I'd booked online. "Yes, this'll be great", I said. I have no idea why I said that, except that I was very confused. I got a bus into the city centre and started to panic at the thought of being holed up in that space. What had I done?! Pre-autism diagnosis me would have put up with it, annoyed with myself for having made such a stupid decision. Post-diagnosis me got straight on the phone and explained that I'd made a hasty decision and, on consideration, had decided that I would prefer the room I'd booked online.

If I had responded to the panicky feelings of overwhelm and confusion by saying I needed to consider which room to take, I could have avoided wasting my own and the establishment owner's time, but at least, by rectifying the situation as quickly as I could, I managed to avoid spending three nights in a claustrophobic cell.

The example above demonstrates another issue which makes it hard for women with autism to quickly make decisions. We tend to regard things literally and have a difficulty "reading between the lines" and detecting people's motives. By taking things at face value, we can be easily pressured into taking decisions which seem to be based on truth, and which we later realise were based on the other person's agenda. In this case, the hotel owner was subtly giving me a hard sell, highlighting the benefits of the small box of a room which were namely the fact that I could prepare my own food in the small kitchenette and come and go as I pleased. It didn't occur to me until I'd spent half an hour on the bus that I didn't need to prepare my own food (I could either eat at the hospital or there were numerous cafes and takeaways in the vicinity of the hotel) and that I could still come and go as I pleased in the main establishment. It took me a while to realise that the windowless room was charged at a lower rate than the double room I'd booked and it was in the owner's interests to free up the double room during this busy holiday period. These things, which are probably very obvious to other people, don't occur to me until some time after they're presented to me, or until I discuss them with other people.

My example with the hotel owner is quite superficial and was easily rectified, but the lack of understanding about other people's agendas and the resulting feeling of being pushed into saying or doing something which you might later regret can cause real difficulty. When someone has an agenda and you're completely unaware of it, coupled with the fact that you're feeling pressured into responding…it's easy to see how you can make the wrong decisions. These decisions could be connected to significant life questions, from making career choices which don't reflect your needs and interests to staying in an unsupportive or abusive relationship.

Melanie told me about a complicated situation with her father in which she and her sister had the legal right to make decisions about his finances and health care due to the fact that he had dementia. "My sister would make suggestions which, on the face of it, would seem ok. I did my usual and said, 'yeah, that seems fine', and then I'd go away and think about it and start panicking! It dawned on me that my sister's decisions were driven, in part anyway, by a desire to maximise what was coming to her from my father's estate, rather than being driven by what was best for him".

When I asked Melanie how she handled the situation she told me, "I phoned my sister up and just explained that sometimes it takes me a while to get an understanding of what is best in a particular situation and that, having considered it, I felt we needed to explore other solutions for my father's care. I wish I hadn't initially said 'yes' to pretty much everything she suggested, but I did manage to regain control in the decision making process by saying I wasn't happy with the solutions we'd explored so far".

Maureen described her experience of staying with a partner who she was not in love with for five years. "I think I realised early on that I didn't really love him but looking back, he was quite emotionally manipulative. I never understood that he had an agenda and would do all kinds of things to make me stay with him when I tried to leave. I made the wrong decisions for a long time, partly because I was just confused about what was going on".

It wasn't until Maureen was engaged to be married that she ended the relationship. "I felt terrible about changing my mind. I couldn't believe I'd got engaged to him. But it was still the right decision".

Sometimes, changing our minds is embarrassing and feels a bit like holding our hands up and saying, "I got it wrong! I'm a bit daft for doing/ saying what I did!". Changing your mind usually feels terrible in the moment and I've certainly had very cringeworthy feelings when I've done a major life detour. But I've never once regretted changing my mind, no matter how uncomfortable it felt at the time. I've realised now that it just takes me longer sometimes to work out what's right and wrong for me and, if I've jumped in too quick with the wrong assessment, it's always better to turn that around than to sit with it.

Find alternatives to some situations which are never going to work

When you're considering strategies, the good thing is, you can prepare for a future situation based on what has happened in the past and whilst life is always going to throw you some curveballs, there will be some situations which are very similar to previous situations. If you have repeatedly experienced a situation in a negative way, the chances are, this time it won't be any different. It can be difficult to make comparisons from past situations to potential future situations given the fact that they're not exactly the same. What you can work on is recognising the *types of situations* which are problematic and, when a new situation arises, identifying whether or not that is the same *type* of situation – even if the details are different.

Here's an example from my own life. I care about a range of causes and genuinely want to help people, which I hope I do through my writing and client work. However, I always get the feeling that I could be doing more and when I come across an advert for a local charitable organisation looking for someone to be on its board of members, my hand shoots right up! Not only will this be a great way to give back to the community and help make a real difference, I think, it'll also be a good way to meet people. As is my usual, I join and attend the first meeting. I'm exhausted because it's the evening and I remember…I don't function well in the evening and I can't stand being in groups of people. So, I leave the group, feeling embarrassed because they then have to find a replacement and I have to avoid the other board members in the street. I have now learned, after many such experiences, that I should never, ever be on a board of members for a community group because I'm not going to like it and will leave after one attempt. The temptation is still there, the quickening of my heartbeat when I see an ad on a local Facebook page, but now I know to resist it.

Sometimes, it's useful to push ourselves beyond our comfort zone, particularly if there are benefits in doing so. We often view "avoidance" as a behaviour which is undesirable as it leads to us limiting our options. For many people, pushing through their fears and discomfort will take them to a point of realising that they do have the skills to deal with situations and, once they've exposed themselves to those situations, their fears and worries subside. When you have autism, however, you may be confronted with some situations which *never* become better for you; no matter how often and how hard you try to push yourself. This is because it's not a case of simply pushing yourself to confront a difficult situation and experiencing a response which isn't as bad as you thought, which then encourages you to push yourself again. It's a case of recognising there are some situations which simply put so much strain on you that you are best to explore alternatives.

Many women experience a sense of panic when they attempt to change the way they do things, even if their past behaviours have caused them issues. It can be difficult to get your head around the fact that, in order to live a more authentic, healthier and happier life, you need to adapt your perspective and behaviours. Some women are concerned that changing in order to meet their autistic needs will limit their life. Somehow, struggling on and on, no matter how damaging it is, seems like a better option than admitting you have autism and need to adjust aspects of your life.

Lorraine told me, "For the first year or so after my diagnosis, I was upset. I knew what I wanted to change, which included stopping trying to do so much socially and concentrating on a small social circle, but I kept thinking that if I gave into the autism, and admitted this is what I needed, that I'd doomed myself to this limited autistic life. It took me a while to realise that I'm exactly the same person I was before I received my diagnosis. I haven't changed, but I can change the way I do things".

Lorraine's insight is an important reminder that you are exactly the same person you were prior to your diagnosis. But armed with the knowledge that you have autism, you can take an empowered and aware stance about meeting your needs.

Enlist support

If any, or all, of the above rings true for you, you may find it useful to enlist the support of someone you trust who can help you work on your personal boundaries and put into place some of the strategies listed. These changes in behaviours can be difficult to implement, especially when they are driven by core beliefs about how you should respond to other people and situations. Not all of your responses are autism-related, of course, and also tie into family and cultural values, in addition to your own personal history so far. Checking in with someone else with regards to taking some time out to make a decision or changing your mind can be very helpful when you find it hard to make a judgement call in the moment.

Exercise:

Identify a phrase which you can say to people when you feel pressured into making a decision.

Identify a phrase which you can say to people when you wish to change you mind about a decision you have made. How would it feel to say this?

Put the above into practice and note what you gained from doing so.

8 EMBRACING YOUR SPECIAL INTERESTS

Like men with autism, women have a strong attachment to their special interests. Having interests isn't a side issue for women with autism. If you have an autistic brain, being able to delve deeply into subjects and find out all there is to know about Victorian architecture, the social life of bees, how the mind works or pottery making is a deep need which, if unmet, can lead to issues including anxiety and depression.

In the journey towards authenticity, it is important to recognise how significant your interests are in terms of who you want to become. Given that, culturally, women continue to take on more responsibility for domestic duties[99], many of the women I work with have left behind things they were once passionate about because they have become involved with work and family duties; falling under the pressure that so many of us do to pay the bills and stay on top of running a household.

Whilst having interests we're passionate about is important to most of us, whether or not we have autism, what comes across in the work I do with women with autism is just *how* important their interests are in terms of how they experience life. This isn't a case of feeling it would be pleasant to "get back into" your special interest. It is a case of feeling that there is something deep and integral missing inside of you. Specialist interests can be regarded as nourishment for the brain. Deny yourself what you're passionate about and you're literally starving your brain.

From my personal experience, I love to research and I love to create in terms of writing. When I was doing my Ph.D., I felt like a completely whole person. Despite being a single mother to a tiny baby when I started, I spent my days reading, researching, putting together facts and figures and creating my thesis. My brain was so well fed, allowed as it was to go deep into research papers and historical documents, that I didn't have the time to feel unhappy or anxious.

After a short stint as an academic, which I didn't enjoy due to the departmental infighting and constraints on my work, I took jobs in middle management which were anything but intellectually demanding. Eventually, I established my own business as a therapist and soon began teaching and, after a long journey, reached the point where I could, once again, combine my client work with conducting research and creative output.

During the years where I had let this side of me slip, regarding it as less important than paying the bills, I lost myself. My anxiety, depression and addictions threatened to overtake me at times. I now know that I *need* this. I *need* to research, explore and create. Without that in my life, I can't be fulfilled.

What feeds your brain?

This can be a difficult question to answer, especially if you have, over the years, ignored those passions and interests which might have once meant a lot to you.

It is worthwhile considering that those things you find interesting may not be things which the vast majority of people find interesting (although they may be). People with autism are often drawn to subjects and interests which are quite niche in nature, although women with autism tend to display less "niche" interests than men. What is significant for both men and women with autism is the *intensity* of interest in their passion.

When it comes to special interests, there is no right or wrong. Perhaps you like playing computer games, or watching documentaries, or decorating cakes or walking up hills. Perhaps you like having time out to read books or collect fabric. What your brain needs is unique to you. But whatever those needs are, it is important for you to nurture and feed your brain in the right way.

There are no weird interests

Many women with autism have been told, often since childhood, that their interests are weird or inappropriate. Because the interests of women with autism may not conform to more traditionally female stereotypes, they can be considered as abnormal, which can contribute to the lack of effort which women put into pursuing them later in life. The intensity with which women pursue their interests can also lead to an assumption that their interests are weird.

"I have this passion for history. I never studied it, but I just love reading history books, collecting stuff, visiting museums – you name it. I was like that even as a kid and my siblings would all make fun of me. They thought I was very weird and I tried to hide my interest as I got older", Jo told me.

"I genuinely have no interest whatsoever in hearing about other people's kids' teething and potty training issues. I know my children will go through this. All kids do. Why do we need to talk about it? I want to talk about the psychology of cats, which I could talk about all day. But I can see people looking at me blankly at the school gates!", Alison said.

Jenny related how her family laughed at her interest in butterflies and her father told her it made her seem odd. "We lived next to a butterfly farm and I became totally obsessed. When I was little, my dad loved to take me there a lot and we had a season ticket. Then he became fed up with my level of interest. He told me it was strange and that other people would think I was odd and I was stopped from going. I was so upset that I lost interest, until recently".

Caroline, similarly, thought other people were right when they categorised her extreme interest in her favourite band, at the age of 50, as very odd. "I know most people grow out of their obsession with a band. Especially when you're a woman it seems pretty odd to buy all the limited releases, keep up to date with all their social media, save up and see them as often as you can. I don't have any friends who act like that".

How do you manage your special interests?

One problem which often presents itself is how women manage their special interests in a way which allows them to manage their other responsibilities, including work and family life. Some women's special interests become their work, or they develop such an interest in their area of work that this becomes their special interest – even if that wasn't the case previously.

Nora told me that, as a child, she had been fascinated with making boxes. "I presume other people thought it was a phase but I kept on doing it. At art school, I did this incredible box like structure for my final presentation and I've been kind of doing variations on the same theme for over twenty years! People pay me a lot of money now for my boxes, which are the most extravagant, complicated boxes you can imagine".

Adrienne described how, although she'd had no particular interest in waste management before starting her current post, she was now obsessed with it. "I'm not really interested in one thing, as such, but what interests me – obsesses me – is the process of research. This project I'm working on is very different to my previous research interests but if you set me on any topic, I'll become completely and utterly obsessed with it".

Sophie turned her obsession with fabric into a profitable business. "I love collecting pieces of fabric, including antique fabric. I've done this since I was a kid. I loved the feel, the smell and the look of it, it just fed my senses. Now I have an online shop selling all around the world".

Not everyone, however, wants or manages to turn their special interest into a business or works in a field which feeds their brain in this way. For some women, managing their special interest causes a conflict when it comes to combining their interest with their other roles.

Maureen told me, "I find it impossible to multi-task and I'll sit for hours reading books about ecosystems. I want to find out everything. I'll end up searching on the internet well into the night. I've woken up absolutely exhausted and had to go to work, but I can't stop myself in the moment".

Heather felt that her special interest in painting ceramic models impinged on the time she spent with her children. "I feel terrible sometimes. I'm ok with the fact that I've got a hobby but it goes way beyond that for me. I can feel really annoyed that I've got to drag myself away from my ceramics to attend to my own kids. I literally would happily sit there all evening, every evening. Sometimes I feel like a terrible mum".

Achieving that balance, then, between having a special interest which is essential to your wellbeing and being able to manage it so that you have time and energy for any other responsibilities you have in life can be difficult. If your special interest is also your career, or if you have fewer responsibilities, getting that brain nourishment may be easier. It's important though, to remember, that even if pursuing a special interest which is important to you does conflict with some of your other roles in life, it's worth making the effort to somehow carve out time and space for yourself to feed your brain. This may involve enlisting the support of those around you and voicing how important it is for your mental health to have time to pursue your interests. It may involve timetabling in particular times of days that are ringfenced for your interests and, if possible, creating a space which is your own. This process starts with the recognition that you need this time for you – whatever shape it might take.

Exercise:

Identify a time in your life when you have felt that you are receiving the "brain food" that you needed. What were you doing that made your brain feel alive and nurtured?

What was it about that previous experience which fed your brain? Was it the ability to become immersed in something? Was it learning a new skill? Was it pursuing a creative output? Was it the creation of order through collecting or cataloguing?

How can you currently incorporate elements of what your brain needs into your current life? You may find yourself doing something quite different to what you have done in the past but in a way which meets your needs.

What do you have to do in order to ensure you will incorporate this interest/ passion into your current life? (Identify the practical steps, such as timetabling an activity or creating a space in which to pursue it, which you need to put into place).

9 PURSUING AN AUTHENTIC CAREER

Many of us have careers which don't fully meet our needs. This is true for people whether they have autism or not. Differences in education, societal expectations and opportunities, combined with a need for financial security means that many people fall into roles which are unfulfilling and stressful. If we're fortunate enough to be in a position where we have a good school education and, perhaps, have the possibility of going to college or university which opens up alternative possibilities for us career wise, we're starting off from a fairly good point.

Our initial steps into considering a career path are usually in our late teen years. This will be partly based on our performance at school, partly based on our family's expectations and partly based on our own preferences. Many people feel pressured in certain directions at this age and women with autism are no different. Many of my clients describe how they felt pushed into career choices, often influenced by the opinions of family members, which became unfulfilling later in life. Given the overwhelm that women with autism face when confronted with choice and the naivety of many girls with autism, they may be particularly quick to listen to the opinions of other people when it comes to embarking on a career.

Having autism makes it far harder for people during those years when they are making choices to make the types of choices which are right for them career wise. It also means, if they have made the "wrong" choice, that they will face considerable difficulties as a result.

Women with autism face inherent problems with social issues, emotional regulation and sensory processing. However, they may not fully realise the extent of these problems until they are some way into their career. Going to college or university can be a terrifying ordeal for autistic women, where the rules and structure of school are replaced with new ways of being.

Sandy told me, "I was very bright at school. I never fitted in but I did have one friend and I was ok with that. I went to university and it was way too much. I couldn't handle the social side and used to hole up in my room the whole time. I was so lonely. Eventually I attempted suicide and my parents took me home. That was the end of university for me".

Jada described the extreme anxiety she felt at college. "I was worried all the time. I was too scared to ask questions or ask for help. I started drinking heavily and using drugs and I got through, but I found it a horrible time of life".

Alison told me that, "I always had an issue at school. I was badly bullied and I bunked off as much as I could. Nobody bullied me at college but I was just left out. People didn't seem to like me and I had no idea what was expected of me. I seemed to feel a lot younger than the other girls".

In the workplace, many women struggle with coming to terms with the difficulties they face in comparison to their colleagues and continue to pursue careers which don't fit with their needs. If everyone else manages fine in this work environment, surely you have the problem, right? Wrong! Just because everyone else does fit into that work environment (although you never actually know what types of struggles your colleagues may be facing behind the scenes) doesn't mean that you will *ever* comfortably fit into that work environment.

Does this mean that, in order to feel fulfilled and comfortable in the type of work you do, you need to leave your current job? Not necessarily. What it does mean, though, is that you can explore this issue from a different perspective. Instead of thinking, "Everyone else manages this aspect of the job which means I should be able to do the same", you could start to consider it from this perspective. "There are some aspects of my job which I find harder because of my autism. How can I adapt some of my work practices to accommodate my needs?".

For some women, this question might lead to the answer that, actually, it is impossible to adapt your current work to the extent that it can support your needs. For other women, who are happy with some aspects of their work but find others difficult, it may mean seeking out support and directing your energies into those aspects of the job which you find satisfying and which you are good at. Many of us spend so much of our lives working that our experience in the workplace has a major impact on all aspects of our lives, including our mental and physical health, relationships and finances.

An authentic career is one in which we feel we have a sense of purpose, in which we can utilise our skills and bring aspects of our true selves into our work selves. Having autism means that when things aren't going quite right, in the workplace or in any other part of your life, you're likely to experience this deeply. Whereas someone without autism may have more of an ability to compartmentalise the fact that their job is not their dream career choice, someone with autism might find themselves becoming emotionally overwhelmed and unable to separate what is happening at work from what is occurring in other aspects of their lives.

All of these factors combine to create a career path which may be punctuated by stops and starts, gaps and changes in direction. Many women find themselves taking on similar jobs to those which have already caused them problems, often out of necessity, and being unable to continue working in these positions for a variety of reasons.

Jenny told me that, "I always, always struggle at work. I seem to have about an eighteen month shelf life. It's usually because

I've fallen out with someone in management. I can't stand seeing injustice and I always end up kicking up a fuss and then having to leave".

Diana repeatedly tried to pursue a career in sales, even though she found herself leaving positions after a few months to a year. "I had this vision of having this career. I want to have a good lifestyle and there are plenty opportunities in the field I'm in. I've had a few jobs but I always end up coming up with an excuse about being ill, or having to care for a family member, because I get to the point where I can't cope with the pressure. Then I get a new job with a different company and it always ends up the same. These environments I work in are so competitive, there's so much sucking up to people and you need to be able to socialise out of work. I can't do it".

Danielle pursued a career in design and, despite loving the creative aspect of her job, found dealing with clients extremely difficult. "I guess I took a CBT approach to the whole thing, and actually visited a therapist in connection with it. She told me that if I kept exposing myself to the aspects of work I found really difficult – such as making the initial client calls and trying to sell them my services – it would get better. But it never did. The stress I faced was always the same and I would be wiped out all day after contacting a client. I've realised I need some kind of job without that sales aspect in it".

Nora pursued a career in teaching and found the sensory overload of being in the school was too much to cope with.

"Everything, from the lights, to the smell of disinfectant, to the noise of the kids — not to mention the social stuff I face with my colleagues — was too much for me. I was exhausted and on the verge of a breakdown and I had to leave".

The inability to secure employment which fits with their needs is a source of great distress for some women who have had to depend on their partner or parents for financial support, and the inability to hold down a job can severely impact a woman's self-esteem.

Mary told me, "I've had so many opportunities and each job I've messed up. I just think I'm such a failure. This is something that everyone else can do".

Tonya similarly saw herself as a failure. "I'm 'working' now, running a business, but it's not much more than a hobby really. I couldn't survive unless my husband paid the bills. I could never work nine to five again. That's not even a choice. I just couldn't do it. At least what I'm doing now gives me happiness".

It's so important to remember that, no matter how unconventional or chaotic your career history might be, or how much you struggle in the position you're currently in, there's a reason for it. I have a similar history of chopping and changing jobs and, prior to running my own business, the longest I'd ever stayed in one job was eighteen months. I went through a phase of being very down on myself. I'd had some really great career opportunities and I'd thrown them all away because of anxiety, being unable to deal with office politics, feeling overwhelmed all the time and having a deep-rooted fear of public speaking (which was required in the field I worked in). When I saw friends carving out successful careers, I wondered why I hadn't been able to do so when we'd all got similar qualifications. I know now that there are some careers which will never be right for me, no matter how hard I try. When it comes to my own business, there are certain facets which I need to outsource or avoid altogether because of the stress they would cause me. Far from keeping on keeping on, I recognise the impact of taking on roles which are damaging to me and put even greater effort into having a manageable and fulfilling career.

Exercise:

What areas of your current (or last) job do you struggle with most? Can you see how these difficulties relate to autism?

Take a look at your career history. Can you see patterns in terms of why you have left particular positions? Were your reasons for leaving due to emotional reasons, social interactions, overwhelm or an inability to carry out specific tasks associated with the position?

Drawing on your values and your needs, what would help you to move to a point of authenticity in your career?

10 BECOMING YOUR AUTHENTIC SOCIAL SELF

Many women initially question whether they have autism, and seek help, because of the difficulties they face socially. One of my earliest memories of feeling very uncomfortable socially was on my third birthday. I was having a nice time alone with my mother, when my grandmother turned up with my three cousins and a friend of theirs from nursery. I remember the horror, fear and anger which welled up in me. I grabbed a tea cosy and put it on my head – I had a thing for hats at the time – and I ran around the house screaming "Get them out!" until they left. My cousin, who was only six months older than me, asked my mum if I was "daft". That same sense of having my whole day ruined by too many people being present is something which I have experienced my whole life. The desire to cover my head and run around yelling, "Get them out!" is as strong as it was when I was three, but I learned to camouflage any sense of discomfort around groups of people and relied on alcohol for many years to make myself be more outgoing and to be able to cope with the anxiety of social situations.

Having a rewarding social life as a woman with autism is extremely hard. We're driven to be social, yet experience the world in a way which makes that particularly tough. How do you explain to someone that although you like them, you don't want to meet their friends or family or go with them on a camping trip which involves another couple? For me, one or two friends at a time is plenty. I would happily sit for hours with the same person, chatting away, drinking and eating, with no desire to go anywhere or meet anyone. It was the same when I was in a relationship. I would feel so happy with the object of my affections that it wouldn't come into my reckoning to leave the house or meet up with other people. Early on, I realised that this could be quite annoying for other people. I may not have had the desire to socialise with more than one person at a time, but I did have self-awareness.

I made up my own rule book. It took me years to perfect and it was edited and re-edited in response to yet another social situation where I said or did the wrong thing. I learned things like:

- Look someone in the eye when you're talking to them
- Ask people about themselves
- Don't stare off into space when the talk turns to kids or handbags
- Don't make inappropriate jokes until you know someone well

- You can butt into a conversation if you wait for a break

- Don't laugh at offensive things

- Smile and nod when you've completely lost track of the conversation

- Take a moment or two to respond if you're confused when asked a question

And so, I passed as "normal". A bit on either the quiet or the mad side depending on who was giving an account, but definitely in the normal sphere. The friends-of-friends, family members and in-laws didn't see the amount of effort that went into socialising and the exhaustion which I experienced after a few hours of being "on". What always upset me was when someone called me out for being "the quiet one" and, on a few occasions, for "looking depressed" when I'd been putting so much effort into being sociable and trying hard to look like I was enjoying myself.

Since my diagnosis, I have done two things in the pursuit of a more authentic social me. Firstly, I am comfortable saying no to events which I know are going to drain me (possibly for days). When I can't say no, or when I'm looking forward to seeing people for a short amount of time, I have learned to set strict limits on the amount of time I will spend in any social situation. Often, I do enjoy the first hour or so of a party or get together, and then I've had enough and the weariness and overwhelm set in. I now say that I have to be somewhere else at a given time and have clear time limits. Another thing which has helped me to become more authentic is to be more comfortable in displaying my quieter self. I no longer put on an act every second. Instead, I ask questions which are interesting to me and which many people might like to be asked; those deeper types of questions about how someone is feeling or what their experience has been like recently. I have realised that people can be very open to someone who perhaps isn't following all the expected (and inherently limiting) social norms.

For Maureen, realising that she didn't have to aim to be the most socially outgoing person in a room was key in her pursuit of social authenticity. "I think because I felt awkward and uncomfortable growing up, I over-compensated and learned how to be Miss Popular, even though I was dying inside. I aimed to be the loudest, the brashest, the funniest person in the group. I sort of always played a part. Now my goal is to be sociable and nice and feel comfortable, without aiming to be super-confident and outgoing".

Melanie told me, "I've always seen myself as an unsocialised dog which needs muzzled. I've decided to let a bit of my 'unsocialised dog' out! I know I'm too much for some people but I know other people like me because I'm a bit out there. I've realised you can't please all the people all the time, and I've spent a long time trying to do that. I let more of myself show now and if someone doesn't like it, they can choose to be with someone else".

For Kelly, she didn't feel she could ever be totally socially authentic, but she did feel she had learned enough to get by socially, whilst protecting her "real" self. "Not many people know me. And that's ok. I have my husband and sons, one or two close friends. I've got my checklist of what to say and do socially but I've accepted I'm just not really interested. I don't want many other people in my life. As long as I can get through social situations, that's ok. I don't feel a need to 'reveal' the real me to people whose opinion I'm not really fussed about".

For Tonya, part of the solution lay in clearly identifying what she did and did not want to get involved in socially. "I think I've done such a good job of looking quite happy at social events, and because I drink heavily I can usually think of something to say to people, that nobody knows how uncomfortable I am. And so I get invited to things and I say 'yes'. Part of me feels flattered that other people think I'm normal enough to have along! I go and I hate it and wish I was at home. I'm learning to say no now, to work out where I actually want to be".

Like Tonya, many women with autism are grateful to be included socially because they feel that they are "weird" and may have a history of being excluded during their teenage years due to difficulties in understanding the complexities of the social lives of teenage girls. Women with autism are rarely "mean girls" and they don't understand how people with an agenda operate. Because of this, they may fail to pick up on who wants what from someone else and the game playing which can occur as girls pursue more complex social agendas.

"I genuinely had no idea what was going on in college. One day, I was ostracised from the group. I didn't know why. It had something to do with some guy I liked and I didn't know some other girl liked him too, and then her friends treated me like an enemy. Anyway, I didn't know how the group worked until I had no friends for the rest of the term", Jo told me.

Women with autism often see things in black and white terms and can be blunt and to the point in their means of expression. When you're like this, it's not only hard to keep track of social complexities, but easy to say or do the wrong thing within that social group. This is why so many girls with autism find themselves confused when friendships change and they're suddenly no longer part of a group, sometimes for failing to follow the social "rules".

Diana explained the desire that so many women with autism feel to be part of a group of popular girls, and how this desire can carry on into adulthood. "After 20 years of no contact, one of the girls from a group I hung about with at university contacted me on Facebook. I immediately thought, great, they want to be friends! We had a zoom meeting and it was horrible. I had no more in common with them now than I did then, and the ones who had kept in touch over the years seemed to have plenty bitchy to say behind each others' backs. I don't know why I thought it would be a good idea. It was awful! Thankfully,

I feel like I'm old enough now to see it for what it was".

Can you be authentically social in the type of group Diana describes above? And, if not, how do you cope with it? In an ideal world, we would be able to be part of social groups where we feel comfortable enough to be ourselves and to mix with other like-minded people. In reality, whether we're required to socialise within families who are very different to us, or whether we need to maintain good social relations at work, we can't always choose which groups we are a part of.

When you're in these situations, you need to discover how much of your authentic self it is appropriate and safe to share with others. Becoming authentic means that you are true to yourself; it doesn't mean that you need to share every aspect of that true self with everyone else. Given the rigid and "black and white" thinking which is often a characteristic of autism, there is sometimes a tendency to think that the opposite of masking and camouflaging is to go out there with everything on show, whilst having little regard as to how this will impact you.

On your journey towards social authenticity, you are in charge. You're not pushed into hiding the real you. And you're not pushed into revealing the real you. You're not pushed into doing anything at all, in fact. This isn't an all or nothing situation and you're not going to know how it feels to be socially authentic until you begin trying out different ways of being to see how they fit. Some might fit better than others.

Making this judgement call about what feels right for you

socially extends to whether or not you choose to share your autism diagnosis, and with whom. Some of my clients have felt pressured into sharing their diagnosis with everyone, as soon as they discover they are autistic. Whilst this may be appropriate for some people, and some women take on the role of autism advocate once they have been diagnosed, other women feel that it has left them in a vulnerable position.

Josie told me, "As soon as I was diagnosed, I shared it with pretty much everyone. I don't know why, but I sort of felt like that was the right thing to do. I had a horrible experience at work recently when I'd had problems with a difficult client. I'd stayed professional throughout but my senior colleague apologised to my client and told them I was autistic as a means of explaining my behaviour. I felt ashamed, betrayed and deficient".

Melanie echoed what so many women with autism experience when they share their diagnosis. "People just told me I didn't seem autistic at all. I found it a deflating experience sharing my diagnosis. I wish with hindsight I'd taken my time and shared it as and when it seemed safe to do so".

Everyone, no matter whether they have autism or not, has a "social self" which differs between the various groups we belong to. The problem is, you may be hiding aspects of your personality which would help you a lot if you shared them. You may also go through life feeling unheard and unknown because you have created such a thick veneer over who you really are when you are around other people. You may have some interesting points to make in work meetings but are afraid to speak up because you feel overwhelmed and avoid speaking at all instead of risking saying the wrong thing. You may sense that the quieter person at a social gathering might like to talk about something other than the banal conversation which is going on around you, but lack the courage to reveal that you are also like that.

The concept of what a friend is can be challenging for some women with autism[100] and many have problems knowing what is expected of them in friendships, for instance, in terms of how to provide and show support and in desiring the exclusive attention of a particular, and sometimes only, friend[101]. Some women find the complexity of female friendships too difficult to navigate and find friendships with men "easier".

The complexities involved in determining how to become more authentically social tie in closely to what it means to establish healthy boundaries between yourself and others, which can be problematic for women with autism. Many of the women I work with have a hard time in establishing safe boundaries for themselves, partly stemming from their confusion about what is right and wrong and a tendency to take things literally. When women have, in the past, experienced a negative reaction to what others might consider an over-stepping of boundaries, they have sometimes gone to the other extreme and have found it very hard to identify or establish healthy boundaries. Some women are so concerned about upsetting other people that they completely fail to prioritise their needs and feel pushed into social situations which are extremely damaging for them.

Sheila described Christmas with her wife's family. "It's a nightmare for me. We stay for a week, camped up in the basement. Her family's huge and there's constant socialising, games, all that stuff. I don't get any alone time and I usually end up having a meltdown at some point. It takes me over a week to recover".

When I asked Sheila whether she had spoken to her wife about the effect this was having on her, she replied that she felt guilty about raising the issue. "I just don't feel I can say no to any of the stuff they want to do, no matter how badly it affects me. I feel like I'm the difficult, odd one", she told me.

Jada described the constant pressure she felt from her cousin, who had recently moved closer to where Jada lived. "I was so happy initially when she moved nearer, but she's been becoming more and more dependent on me. I'm often totally exhausted after working all week but Rhia always wants to do something at the weekend, or she wants my husband and I to go round and help her out. And I just can't say no".

Establishing healthy boundaries between yourself and others is difficult for most people and is closely linked to how you were raised and cultural expectations about acceptable behaviour, including gendered expectations. Women with autism often face an additional internal pressure to please others by saying yes to social demands because of the fear of being lonely and excluded, which they may have experienced at times in their past. When you add this to the confusion experienced when requested to do something and difficulties in accessing the logical, thinking part of the brain when an emotional response is triggered, it's understandable that creating healthy boundaries is particularly difficult for women with autism. In addition to putting into place the strategies outlined above, including taking time out to think over a request, saying no and asking for the opinion of someone you trust, you may also need to shift your perspective. Particularly if you have experienced rejection in the past or you suffer from low self-esteem, you may currently think that you are obliged to meet everyone else's demands because you're the one who is "different" or "difficult" and that, if you don't agree to this person's demands, you might end up socially isolated. At the end of the day, your social needs might be different to other people around you, but you need to honour that fact. That doesn't mean being friendless, but it does mean working out how to meet your own needs within the context of friendships which are supportive and to develop strategies for meeting your own needs within situations which are more demanding.

Jada spent a considerable amount of time working on establishing healthy boundaries with her cousin and, by doing so, was able to maintain a healthy relationship. "What's happened in the past with friends and family is that I've bent over backwards for everyone and I end up exhausted. The only solution has been to cut myself off completely. With Rhia, I've learned to say no. It feels horrible, but I've forced myself to set some boundaries and I hope that'll allow us to stay close without me burning out".

Although it required a huge amount of effort, Sheila discussed with her wife ways in which she could protect herself during the Christmas visit to her wife's family. "I was upset when I was doing it, but I just pointed out that I really need alone time when I'm in a situation like that. It doesn't mean I don't like her family but I cannot deal with being around that level of noise and chaos. I spent some time alone each day reading while the rest of them did stuff that I hate, like board games, and it helped me so much. Instead of feeling I was being too demanding in asking for that, I felt like it was something I had to do to look after myself".

Setting boundaries is tough and it's important to know that you're not being self-indulgent or selfish in doing so. What you are doing is looking after yourself and respecting your needs. So what if your needs are a bit different to other people's? That doesn't make them any lesser. It's also possible that what is holding you back from creating healthy boundaries is an unfounded worry about how your requests will be met. Rumination is commonly experienced by people with autism[102] and women with autism often ruminate on the quality of their social experiences, sometimes coming to conclusions which don't reflect the reality of the situation. This also stems back to difficulties in working out what is going on for other people, which can lead to excessive worry that setting healthy boundaries will have negative effects. Many of the women I work with express a desire to establish healthy boundaries which appear to be perfectly reasonable, but which are perceived by them as having the potential to provoke a strong negative response.

Melanie told me about a change in working systems at work which meant that she now had more paperwork which was causing her so much stress that she was unable to perform her usual duties which formed the core of her work. When I suggested that she might raise this with management, she felt it would be received very negatively. After talking it through, and remembering that she worked for a health board who valued neurodivergence, she realised that she had worried so much about saying anything that she had lost sight of the reality of the situation.

Jo, similarly, realised that her difficulty with establishing healthy boundaries was partly due to the extreme worry and rumination she experienced after social interactions. "I'll come home and spend hours thinking about whether I said or did something wrong. I can be up all night worrying that one particular word offended someone. The thought of saying no to someone worries me so much it's just easier to say yes all the time".

There is no one way to be more authentically social. What's important to remember as you move forwards socially is that you are in charge. There's no time pressure and you can experiment with how you bring yourself to different social situations. What feels right and appropriate? How can you look after yourself whilst enjoying a richer social experience? How do you meet *your* needs within social groups? Experimenting with being more socially authentic allows you to discover what feels right and wrong for you and to develop strategies for meeting your social needs.

11 AUTISM AND GENDERED DISCOURSES

During one therapy session, before my autism diagnosis, I raised an issue with my counsellor which had been apparent to me for a long time, and which made little sense to me. "I don't feel like a *woman*", I said. I could see that my therapist looked a bit puzzled. I was a woman in my forties with a long-term male partner and two children. I suspect I conformed to fairly stereotypical "female" expectations in terms of appearance and lifestyle choices, including my choice to establish my own business so that I could be there for the school and nursery pickups. I didn't know what I meant by what I was saying, either. I'd considered this issue over the years and only came up with conflicts. I had a history of having female friends, I always wanted to have children, I had long hair and liked fairly feminine clothes ("fairly" being the operative word here – no high heels or anything too glamourous). I'd never been what you'd call a "Tomboy". I was quite envious of tomboy types, but it wasn't me. And yet, I kept coming back to this point. I didn't feel like a woman.

After my autism diagnosis, I revisited this issue and I realised that my not identifying with being a woman had more to do with the fact that it was hard for me to identify with socially expected female behaviours. I examined the female friends I had. Those friendships tended to be shaped around shared interests or they were formed with friends who also didn't fit into stereotypical female roles.

When I became a mother, I found the whole mothers' social scene unbearable. I loved my baby but I had absolutely no interest in spending time with other mums discussing bowel movements and dietary requirements. I'd go along to a toddlers' group and feel the life drain out of me. I eventually learned what the conversation topics were and how to initiate a conversational thread about the pros and cons of breastfeeding but I just couldn't face putting in the effort. I was too tired from sleepless nights to have the energy to keep putting myself out there. I'm sure there were some women equally bored and frustrated, but the majority, it seemed to me, appeared to naturally know how to have chats about their children's food preferences. I couldn't do it and ended up making absolutely no "mummy friends". I discussed this with a male work colleague once who called me "pretentious", totally missing the point that I was desperately craving company but felt like I was a different species the second I entered the mums' scene.

My confusion over why I didn't feel like a woman was, I think, in large part the result of feeling uncomfortable in groups of women. I like women on a one-to-one basis but a group of women isn't a tribe I can easily identify with. I think it also came from just not having any interests in some things which many women identify with. Because of how I viewed myself, I was always genuinely surprised when other people saw me as a woman. I always assumed that other people would see me as "other", because that is how I felt. I was very surprised one year when someone gave me a nail polish set as part of a Secret Santa family in-laws gift. I was quite flattered that someone had seen me as a "normal" woman who might appreciate such a girly gift.

Since my diagnosis, I have more of an understanding about this feeling of disconnect and have realised that so much of it is down to measuring myself against neurotypical women and feeling different. My feelings of disconnect never caused me any great discomfort but it has been useful for me to come up with an explanation as to why I experienced them. It's also helped me be less hard on myself for having found it hard to make female friends in the context of traditionally female contexts, such as mother and toddler groups or school pick-ups. I used to get annoyed with myself for not making more of an effort, but now I have a greater appreciation that the energy of trying to fit in was probably just too much for me. For me, those mum-kid type environments are extreme high-pressure social settings which take so much energy that I can feel ill for days afterwards. Choosing to distance myself from them was undoubtedly the right choice at the time, even though it felt like I was missing out.

One study revealed that, whilst some women rejected gender based theories of behaviours, others felt a strong pressure to conform to more stereotypical gendered roles[103]. Conforming to some of these roles, such as "wife" or "girlfriend" had, at times, led to a sense of a loss of identity[104].

Marianne told me about the pressure she felt to conform to a role which just didn't "fit" her. "For a while, because I had two small kids and we could afford it, I chose to be a stay-at-home mum. It was such a difficult time in my life. I felt this pressure to be a perfect stay-at-home-mum and yet the whole lifestyle didn't sit with me. I stopped doing all the things I enjoyed and suffered a complete breakdown".

Tonya expressed a discomfort with the term, "wife". "I was never keen when people referred to me as Martin's girlfriend – I preferred the term partner because it was non-gendered. And now I find the word 'wife' just sort of gives me the creeps. I love being married to him, I just don't like thinking of myself as a wife or using that term".

Maureen told me, "I never gave much thought to gender, really, before I had kids but I have this idea of what a mum is and have trouble identifying with it. I love my kids but I've got a sense I'm different to all the other mums I meet".

Caroline explained how difficult she found being a mother, and how this led to a sense of disappointment in herself as a woman. "I know a lot of mums struggle, but I'm sure most of them don't struggle as much as I do. I have to go to bed sometimes during the day, because I can't cope with the noise and mess anymore. I feel like a complete failure as a mother and as a woman".

Similarly to my own experience, many women's perception of themselves in relation to gender is heightened at particular times in life, including teenage years and when they form long term relationships or become mothers. Some women, post-diagnosis, discover that their issues with identifying with traditional female roles is linked to their difficulty in identifying with neurotypical people, regardless of gender.

Marie told me, "There was a time when I just didn't feel like a woman. I couldn't explain why exactly – I just felt different from the other women I knew. But I didn't feel like a man, either. I realised when I was diagnosed with autism that I just didn't feel like the other people I knew, male or female. I've got a tribe now of like-minded women".

Some women also express a preference for male company, especially when it comes to being in groups of men. Many women find it easier to join in with male conversations, which may be based more around specific interests than to follow conversations in groups of women which may involve more social complexities.

Annabelle described how, at family parties, "I always end up chatting to the blokes. I find it so much easier. They'll get onto talking about films and music, which I love. If they move onto sports I can just zone out and they don't notice. If I was with a group of women and I zoned out for a bit one of them would be concerned and ask me what was wrong!".

There is some evidence that having autism increases the likelihood that a person may not identify with their assigned-at-birth gender, a condition known as gender dysphoria[103], or that they may reject a binary gender identity[104]. A high proportion of my younger clients – those under the age of 30 – have expressed a degree of gender dysphoria and a rejection of binary gender identity. The fact that my clients over 30 don't tend to express the same experience or use the same terms may point to the fact that they have grown up in a different era when the discourse around gender was more limited along with potential means of identifying and expressing one's gender.

Simone told me, "I'm not sure I ever felt like a woman, when I looked at other women around me, but I would have lacked the language to express this in any way. I also assumed, when I was a young woman, that if you were heterosexual there were no other discussions to be had around the subject. I hear the expression non-binary now and it's something I want to find out more about".

Yvonne mentioned that, "I've always sort of gravitated towards women who have strong feminist views and a few of my friends were gay or bisexual. I suppose I had questions around whether or not I felt like I conformed to this image of what a woman should be – I certainly hated many of the trappings associated with femininity – but I've never used any terms or language to express that".

In contrast, younger women increasingly have a narrative which enables them to express their discomfort with, or rejection of, stereotypical categories.

Ade told me that she rejects the term "woman" in favour of Assigned Female at Birth (AFAB). "I've always felt that gender is too limiting. I don't feel like a woman and I don't want to identify as a woman. AFAB allows me the freedom to release myself from those limitations and experiment with my gender and sexuality".

Debs explained her perspective on gender dysphoria. "From a young age, I didn't identify as a girl. I was a total tomboy. But I never wanted to be a boy, and I don't want to be a man either. I just don't identify with a strictly female identity".

Jenny explained, "I see people as people. I just don't agree with this idea that we're categorised because we were born male or female. I identify more closely with some men and more closely with some women and I prefer to just think of myself as a person. I don't use a term for that, people can call me female, woman, whatever, but that's how I see things".

Women with autism may also have a tendency to see sexuality as being more fluid, with the idea that sexual orientation can change over time and depending on the situations they find themselves in.

Jane told me, "My boyfriend and I have been together for two years and we're very happy, but I've had relationships with both women and men in the past. I'd identify as bisexual, but that's probably a bit reductive. I don't really see myself as falling into any category. If I fall in love with someone, I don't feel a need to describe that in terms of their gender or my sexuality".

Meghan explained, "I've only ever had heterosexual relationships and I've been married for twenty years but I've never ruled out having a relationship with a woman. It's just something that makes sense to me – that you might fall in love with someone of the same sex".

Whatever the nature of their sexuality and sexual histories, women with autism often express an openness to the possibility of gender fluidity and the acceptance of other people's lifestyle choices which are different to their own.

For some people, it is the embracement of their neurodiversity, and a more open perspective generally to various forms of experience and identity, which leads to an embracement of a non-binary gendered perspective. The discovery that you're neurodivergent can open you up to alternative discourses of what it means to be a person; including alternative gendered discourses.

Toni told me, "I don't feel that I have quite the right term to describe myself yet. But discovering I have autism has made me question my identity more generally, including opening me up to the possibility of a new gender identity".

The link between autism and fluid discourses of gender and sexuality is evident. We're not entirely sure why this link exists and perhaps it's combination of seeing the world differently, rejecting social norms and feeling different to people in general, in addition to feeling a disconnection with people of the same gender. When we take a broad view of the subject, from people who don't identify with roles such as "wife" and "mother" to people who reject binary constructs of gender altogether, we can see that neurodiversity provides the basis for an acceptance and embracement of a pluralistic view of gender.

In terms of leading an authentic life, the more options we have available to us, the better. Having the language to express areas of disconnect and discomfort can only be helpful and having the freedom to explore new ways of expression can all help take us forwards in terms of our personal journey towards authenticity.

12 SELF-CARE AND EMOTIONAL REGULATION

Authenticity is about valuing yourself and respecting your needs. Part of this process involves attending to your self-care needs and managing your emotional regulation needs. Taking on anything new can be difficult when you have autism and lead to feelings of overwhelm and burnout. Exploring what it means to feel more authentic and committing to taking the necessary steps required to make that happen needs to be done in a way which isn't going to feel so overwhelming and exhausting that you fail to embark on the journey.

Self-care involves making a commitment to yourself. Self-care isn't about indulging yourself with behaviours which are essentially self-destructive – such as using alcohol and food to numb difficult emotions. Instead, it's about really taking the time to make contact with yourself. To attend to those emotions which you might find more difficult. And to find ways of nurturing and looking after yourself which show that you value yourself and care about your mental and physical health.

As you move towards authenticity, it requires that you respond to your true needs in an authentic way. Part of this involves putting into place the strategies identified above, such as creating healthy social boundaries and having the courage to say no when you need and want to. It also involves identifying and pursuing your interests and passions. However, let's imagine that you've rediscovered your passion for writing and you're creating the time to pursue that passion by saying no to the numerous demands which your family and friends have been putting on you for the last ten years. That's great, but at the end of the day, perhaps you continue to open the bottle of wine and numb your feelings of anxiety and low self-esteem because they're too painful to get in touch with. You accept that poor sleep is a part of life, skip the exercise and settle into a familiar routine of eating junk food and drinking every night because you cannot look at the discomfort which is a legacy of coping with life with undiagnosed autism.

I would argue that to become more authentic, you need to start looking after your mental and physical needs and that, in addition to being aware of your social needs and making time for interests, this includes digging a bit deeper. Being true to yourself means taking care of yourself.

This is something which many women with autism struggle with. This is partly due to the focused way in which they think and their tendency to become absorbed in a personal or work project. Trying to incorporate self-care into the mix of the other demands in their life can feel like too complicated a juggling act and it requires considerable commitment to do so. Many women find simply dealing with day-to-day demands a real struggle and have very little left in terms of energy to devote to thinking about longer term or bigger issues. One study confirmed the difficulty that girls with autism have with "executive functioning" including the ability to make a plan, follow through with a plan and manage daily tasks such as getting up and dressed[107]. Many of my adult clients similarly experience problems when it comes to managing tasks such as having breakfast, getting dressed, cleaning, and dealing with unexpected work tasks. Taking on the additional task of having a good look at your life and working out where you want to be in the future and the types of steps involved in getting there, in addition to everything else you deal with on a daily basis, can seem overwhelming.

This is one thing which I, like many of my clients, find difficult. I sometimes get up at five in the morning (or earlier) and start work. I might work all day and, unless I need to do the school run, I might not bother getting dressed (I do get dressed if I have clients, however!). I'll eat on the run, work hard, forget to stop for breaks, end up exhausted and wind down with wine and food. This feels to me like a very natural pattern and one which I've been doing since I was at university nearly 30 years ago. I'm dreadful domestically and I find it really hard to do things I have no interest in. Left to my own devices, my kitchen becomes uninhabitable. I am so utterly focused on what I'm working on that I find it very hard to make any time for self-care. I'm well aware of the *need* for self-care, but the implementation requires considerable effort. I have, with a huge amount of effort, managed to improve my attitude towards self-care and, once again, having a strategy in place has been invaluable. If I don't pre-plan, and instead leave it up to "how I feel on the day", I'll be sitting writing until I get repetitive strain injury, and will resort to numbing the physical (as well as mental) pain with a large gin and tonic.

Maureen identified this as a real problem, which she had always experienced. "This is going to sound ridiculous, but one of my main problems is that I can't be bothered eating breakfast. I get up and suddenly my mind has a ton of ideas. Exciting ideas. I can't be bothered even making toast. Then I get really tired, moody…and it impacts my whole day".

Diana recognised the need for self-care and, in particular, getting some exercise outside each day, but expressed a difficulty with getting up and out of the house. "I know I feel so much better if I get out. It changes my mood for the whole day. But then I think of all the stages involved in getting showered, dressed and that whole process can take me ages. By the time I'm ready, I can't be bothered going out".

For Maureen, a workable solution involved having pre-prepared food ready in the fridge for the following morning's breakfast. Diana committed to leaving the house for a walk before showering, putting on the least-effort clothes she could find, and properly showering and dressing following her walk. A useful starting point is to acknowledge that, however easy these things might appear to be, or however easy your partner/ sister/ housemate finds them, they're not easy for you and they're probably not going to become easier. By acknowledging the difficulty involved in carrying out these types of tasks, you can pre-plan and anticipate the types of difficulties you will come up against in advance.

Black and white thinking is another contributor to the difficulty of implementing self-care. Instead of being able to consider self-care, whether that's taking yoga, doing meditation or going for a walk in the middle of the day, as something which can easily be incorporated into your life, many women with autism start to place unreasonable expectations on themselves. They begin to see self-care as having to be the best at something or turning it into a special interest which takes up an unsustainable amount of time. I have experienced this type of thinking. I'll take a yoga class and I need to strive to be the best (which is never, ever going to happen). I'll start having a walk each day and suddenly I'm walking seven miles and it's taking up far too big a chunk of my day to be sustainable. That all or nothing thinking which so many women with autism display can make it very hard to realistically incorporate self-care into a day which has other demands.

One of my clients, Angela, told me how she had enjoyed

doing yoga a few years before she had developed multiple sclerosis. I asked whether this was something she could continue during those times when she felt better – perhaps doing some slow yoga or even practicing from a chair. "No…I was so good, I worked really hard and improved…I'm not going to do it if I can't be as good as I was".

Self-care is important for everyone, and for women with autism, who often have a history of mental health issues, it is crucial.

Anxiety

Many women with autism suffer from anxiety, which is completely understandable when you consider that they have spent their lives navigating their way in a world which doesn't fit with their needs. The world is a confusing place and many of my clients express feelings of overwhelm which can be triggered by a wide range of situations. The autistic brain has a tendency to find it hard to deal with too much information at one time and difficulty in dealing with socially complex situations. This, coupled with sensory overload issues, means that many women find it hard to stay calm in situations. They often find themselves unable to quickly evaluate a situation and, as a result, spend a considerable amount of time caught up in thought loops trying to make sense of situations which they find genuinely confusing. All of this creates anxiety. Many women notice a reduction in anxiety following a diagnosis of autism and an acceptance of their condition. When you become less worried about saying and doing the "wrong" thing, and begin to lead a more authentic life, the triggers for anxiety often reduce. At the same time, it is important to have useful strategies in place to help manage your anxiety whilst you are on your journey towards authenticity.

There are several reasons why women with autism are so prone to anxiety. Firstly, like anyone else with anxiety, it is often rooted in childhood experiences. As children, we learn about our place in the world from our caregivers and the world around us. Women with autism face the same potential situations as does anyone else and may be raised with physically, sexually or emotionally abusive parents. Any child who is criticised, neglected or put down by their parents has the potential to develop anxiety later in life. But having autism adds a whole new dimension to this. First of all, we have the sensory issues. When sounds, tastes, sights, smells and sensations overwhelm and scare you, the world becomes a terrifying place. Simply going to the shops, getting in a car, going on holiday or going to the cinema can be a completely overwhelming sensory experience. So many everyday things can trigger worry and distress. Girls with autism might find it hard to relate to, and communicate with, their parents and other adults and siblings. As a result, they may be misunderstood and ignored, their "difference" meaning they may be left alone. The school playground is a breeding ground for anxiety, when girls may find it hard to make and maintain friendships and may experience bullying due to their differences. School can be overwhelming in many other ways, with the bright lights and noises and verbal instructions. All of these difficulties in childhood can be carried into adulthood as anxiety. When you learn the world and the people in it are threatening and that you don't fit well into it, you carry these beliefs into adulthood.

School was a terrifying place for me from the first day. I remember seeing some children crying and hanging onto the school gates. I remember feeling shocked by this and immediately overwhelmed on entering the school, with its bright lights and strong smell of disinfectant. To me, our teacher, Miss McGregor, was old and scary and I was determined never to upset her. We were told to do our best. I took that literally. I made it my goal to come first in every task we were given and I loved the challenge of getting every single sum right on our little jotters and handing it in before anyone else in the class. I won the prize for "General Excellence" in my first year and kept heaping on the pressure so that I would never slip below my high standards. I loved the order in the classroom; the books, the tests, the spelling and arithmetic. But I couldn't imagine not coming top in all my subjects and I began to buckle under the pressure. I was in a constant state of worry. I was also bullied. I was a fat kid and remember being forced into a stairwell by a group of other kids and asked what I had for breakfast. "Cornflakes", I replied, totally oblivious to the fact I was being bullied. All the children started laughing and saying that I must have eaten a house, or a car...and I blanked out, froze, entered what I now know is a dissociative state. Between the self-induced pressure and the name calling, I began to suffer severe migraines about once a week – usually when it was P.E. day. I was constantly anxious – even outside school I had so many phobias related to sensory stimuli that I didn't like leaving the house – and this anxiety affected me well into adulthood.

Melanie described the anxiety she experienced as a child as, "Being triggered by all kinds of things. The world just seemed too much. I was happy at home, but as soon as I was out there I was scared of noises, traffic and planes, and I was nervous when I was in crowds of people. I just felt this feeling of being scared a lot of the time".

Jo noted the anxiety she experienced within her own family. "I just had a sense that I was different. I lived in quite a big, chaotic, loud family. I would start feeling nervous about what would happen next. Would there be a fight? Would my brother grab me and start tickling me? Just daft things that happen in families, but for me I'd just feel sort of nervous a lot of the time. Worried about what was coming next".

"I was scared stiff at school. Sometimes, I wouldn't understand something – I found it hard to take in verbal information – and then I was terrified about getting it wrong. The teacher said if we were bad we'd get locked in the cleaner's cupboard. I believed this 100%. I'm not sure any of the other kids believed it! It didn't seem to bother them, anyway", Tonya told me.

In a future chapter, I look at the strong connection between autistic women and abuse, which is evident from research[108]. The reasons why women with autism are more susceptible to abuse include: social mimicry; copying a man's flirtatious behaviour without being aware of what you were doing; difficulties in reading the situation; feeling isolated and failing to develop strategies to stay safe; feeling desperate for acceptance due to their experiences of rejection; and uncertainty of social rules and lacking the skills to say "no"[109]. Experiencing this level of trauma earlier in life can be the root cause for anxiety throughout a woman's life.

Social anxiety

Social anxiety tends to be part of the territory for so many women with autism, and it's easy to understand why. Masking aspects of one's personality and being diplomatic are things most people do, to some extent, but women with autism are starting off from a point where they have to put in far more effort to do so. Constantly worrying about doing or saying the right thing is exhausting and anxiety provoking. If you have revealed your "true" self at times, you may have come in for criticism and hurtful comments from others, meaning that all social occasions are minefields. Feeling overwhelmed, confused and drained causes extreme feelings of anxiety. Simply being on the autistic spectrum is, essentially, to be socially anxious; especially when people around you don't understand the difficulties you are facing. Many women are unsure whether their difficulties in social situations are caused by autism or social anxiety. In fact, they are often caused by both given that, if you have autism, you have so many things to think about socially that you become anxious in the process.

Lack of fulfilment

Another common reason for underlying anxiety in women with autism is because they have not fulfilled their purpose and are leading a life which doesn't fit with their values, needs and wants. It's useful to think of anxiety as an inbuilt warning system. We all need it to tell us when something is not "right". For our ancestors, this warning system might have usefully come into play when they were being chased by a tiger or attacked by another tribe. For us, we may become anxious when things just don't feel right; when we're not providing ourselves with what we need in life.

Going back to what we need to feed our brains, so many women with autism are leading lives which don't provide the time and space for them to pursue interests and to carve out much-needed alone time. If you have the type of brain which thrives on fact finding/ collecting/ research or spending time alone or with animals, for instance, and you don't make time in your life to pursue these things, your brain will give you a warning signal that things are seriously not ok. It will let you know that you need to do things differently. We often ignore this built in sense that things aren't right in our lives and we can suffer anxiety as a result.

Emotional regulation

Emotional regulation refers to how we experience our emotions and how we respond to them. We all have emotional responses, many of which are hard-wired into us as human beings. As complex beings, we experience a range of emotions – such as sadness when we lose a person we love or happiness when something positive happens in our lives. Naturally, we prefer some emotions to others (I'm guessing that most of us like the feeling of being happy more than we like the feeling of being anxious). Whilst everyone experiences a range of emotions, how we respond to these emotions will have very different outcomes in terms of our physical and mental health and our quality of life.

When we exercise positive emotional regulation, we have an understanding and awareness of our emotions and the ability to exert a controlled and appropriate response. For instance, instead of screaming at someone who has upset you or punching someone for cutting you off in the road, although you feel the frustration and anger, you manage to exercise control over your emotions. Exercising positive emotional regulation is beneficial to you and those around you. With poor emotional regulation, a whole range of situations will trigger such extreme responses that just being in a meeting at work or picking your child up at the school gates can become trigger loaded activities. People with autism often experience behaviours such as withdrawing, explosive behaviours, outbursts, meltdowns, anxiety, irritability, self-harming and aggression as a consequence of their difficulties with emotional regulation[110].

One of the hallmarks of autism is "meltdowns". Parents of autistic children often describe meltdowns as far more severe than the usual temper tantrums which children often experience. Another way in which meltdowns differ from tantrums is that they are not goal oriented or manipulative and, instead, come from a point of being overwhelmed and lacking the emotional regulatory skills to manage that feeling of overwhelm[111]. Interestingly, although meltdowns is a term commonly used by parents of autistic children, and by autistic adults themselves, this phenomenon has received very little attention in the field of academic research until recently[112].

At a neurological level, why do people with autism have difficulties with emotional regulation? People with autism have a difference in neural structures which are involved in emotional regulation in terms of the size, function and circuitry with other parts of the brain[113]. Research has shown that there is a poor connection between the frontal cortex and the amygdala in people with autism[114]. Put simply, the amygdala can be thought of as an "emotion centre" in our brain; part of our limbic system and our mammalian brain. The frontal cortex can be thought of as our "thinking brain", the more rational part of our brain which makes judgements. Psychiatrist, Steve Peters, refers to the limbic system as our "chimp brain" and the frontal cortex as our "human brain"[115]. The amygdala, which is part of our "chimp brain" works extremely fast to process information and respond to that information. It instantaneously assesses whether something is a threat. At lightning speed, this information is sent to the "human brain" which then assesses that information more rationally. Was that bang in the street really a gun, or was it a car backfiring? When this loop between amygdala and frontal cortex doesn't function as it is designed to, as seems to be the case in people with autism, we can face difficulties making rational judgments and calming our emotional centres. Problems with emotional regulation and associated autism tend to lead to anxiety and depressive symptoms[116,117], externalising behaviours[118-120], poor social functioning[121], lack of success in mainstream secondary classrooms[122] and difficulty with college transition[123]. People with autism are also more likely to receive psychiatric hospitalisation[124].

If having meltdowns has been your experience since childhood, you may well continue to experience meltdowns in adulthood. Meltdowns are an intense emotional response and experiencing a meltdown is horrible. Having a meltdown means that you're out of control, unable to evaluate a situation or think straight and meltdowns can be very upsetting for people around you. The intensity of the emotional reaction to a situation tends to be completely out of proportion to the situation which has triggered that reaction.

I experienced extreme meltdowns as a child. I was usually extremely well behaved. I kept myself to myself and did what I was told. But when I was scared or threatened…it was like unleashing a monster. I couldn't tell you how many doctors' surgeries I attempted to trash and when my mother left me at the hospital when I was due to have my tonsils removed, I experienced a total meltdown. I still remember the absolute feeling of terror and rage (my mum had thought it was a good idea not to tell me I was going to hospital and surprise me with the news when I was standing by the bed with my name on it). I became so violent and scratched mum so badly she ended up with permanent scarring on her hand. I smashed what I could and punched and kicked the nurses. I took hours to calm down. I wasn't allowed any visitors the whole time I was in hospital in case I went "mad" again.

As an adult, to most people, I presented a very contained exterior and made an extreme effort to hide my uncontrollable emotions from people. For instance, when my first boyfriend broke up with me just before my eighteenth birthday, I was devastated beyond belief. I cried all night, I sat piecing together the letter which he had sent and I'd violently ripped up, reading it over and over and over. I screamed when I was alone and spent months (years) sobbing and drinking to the point of blanking out on a regular basis. And nobody in my family even knew I'd been through a difficult breakup. This very extreme emotional reaction has always been a part of my life. Many of the women I work with also experience meltdowns.

Tonya told me, "As a child I would just go mad. I remember having extreme tantrums and my mum tells me that they were very different to my siblings' tantrums. They were far more extreme and could be triggered far more easily. Once, she took me on a walk and I threw myself on the ground, screaming. She couldn't physically get me back into the pram and a neighbour saw and he lifted me into his car and drove us home".

Melanie described the difficulties her meltdowns cause her. "I get so emotional at the slightest things, particularly at work if something goes wrong. I sometimes feel faint, like my head is swimming, I've had to leave work to get home and start yelling and crying. My husband's come home to find me in a complete mess just over a little bit of criticism at work".

Jenny told me that, "I sometimes think of myself as being Jeckyll and Hyde. I'm so guarded around people, I guess some people would describe me as a standoffish. But I go mental when I'm on my own and I'm upset. I bang my head on the wall and actually hurt myself. I cry and cry and rock back and forwards. I feel like I've completely lost the plot when I'm like that".

In addition to causing anxiety and inducing feelings of being out of control, poor emotional regulation has other far-reaching effects.

Jada told me, "My meltdowns were punished so severely when I was little that I've learned to hide any signs of emotion. Other people, including my partner, criticise me for being emotionless and cold, when, in fact, I'm bubbling up with huge emotions inside, which I can't risk letting out".

Andrea described the impact that poor emotional regulation had on her in terms of social interactions. "When I'm upset or frustrated about something, if I go to confront the person who is responsible for that upset, whether it's a shop assistant at a store I'm returning stuff to or whether my partner has said something which offends me, I can't control my emotions. I've started crying and shouting in shops. I often just totally avoid any type of confrontation because I can't trust myself to stay in control".

Jo told me, "There are certain situations which I just can't put myself in. Good and bad. I couldn't have anyone at my wedding because there was a risk of me sobbing uncontrollably with joy. We're not talking sweet crying here, but huge, gulping and snot pouring sobbing. I had to have a wedding with just myself and partner, which wasn't what we really wanted'.

Women sometimes describe feeling a huge build-up of emotion for days and even weeks in advance of an event they're worried about and agree that the build-up is far worse than the actual event.

Tracey described the impact that Thanksgiving had on her every year. "I start getting upset in September. I'll usually start arguments with my husband about his family coming over weeks in advance. I literally end up sobbing for the couple of weeks before hand and it has a huge impact on my work and mental health. I can't focus on anything else when I'm in that state".

Diana described the impact of meltdowns which were usually triggered in the lead up to presentations at work. "If I've got something coming up, usually a presentation which I don't enjoy doing, I'll spend the whole week or so before hand having total meltdowns. Sometimes I've written angry letters of resignation. Thankfully I haven't sent any yet. But I just feel so frustrated and angry, and particularly angry at myself".

Sometimes people react to their meltdowns with a mix of shame and inwardly directed anger. This is particularly the case if other people have been caught up in their meltdown or if they have lost their temper or started crying in public. It's important to remember that, disturbing as it feels to have a meltdown, there's a reason for it. At a sensory and emotional level, you are processing things in a particular way which leads to extreme overwhelm, confusion, fear and frustration. Given that meltdowns are not outcome driven, you're acting in this way because, at that particular time, there doesn't seem to be another available option to you. Feeling ashamed about your actions is simply going to put more pressure on you. But you can learn from the experience and develop strategies to help minimise the impact of future meltdowns. Although you may be starting from a point where emotional regulation is difficult, it is something you can learn to become much better at.

Identify your negative coping strategies

If emotional regulation is an issue for you, it's possible that you have developed some coping strategies which, though perfectly understandable, are actually exacerbating your problems with emotional regulation. Research has shown that people with autism may be more likely to suffer from substance addictions than the general population[125]. This finding was in contrast to earlier assumptions that, because people with autism are often isolated from peer pressure which can encourage experimentation with alcohol and drugs, they are less likely to become addicted to substances[126].

Turning to substances to help manage your emotions is an attractive short-term solution for many people. In the short term, alcohol causes the release of serotonin and endorphins, two "feel good" hormones which can make us feel happy and relaxed. It can help numb the difficult emotions we might be feeling and stop us from ruminating on unhelpful thought loops. In the short term, marijuana can reduce the brain's threat response and can help us feel relaxed, detached, euphoric and happy. Both alcohol, cannabis and other substances, are ways of blunting our experiences and stepping out of ourselves for a time. The long term effects of substance abuse, however, include depression, paranoia and anxiety along with sleep disturbances and health problems. When we become dependent on a substance to regulate our emotions, we have less ability to deal with those emotions ourselves.

If you have been relying on substances to help you manage your emotions, it's important to identify new coping mechanisms which don't have the same harmful side effects and negative long-term effect on your mental health. Identifying what your personal meltdown timeline looks like, enlisting the right type of support, ensuring you get enough rest and engaging in activities which help to reduce your stress levels are all alternatives to relying on alcohol or other substances for emotional regulation. It is advisable to seek the help of your primary care-giver in this process and you may benefit from the help of a suitably qualified therapist or organisation in dealing with substance dependence, if this has been a coping strategy for you.

Ask for support

Meltdowns can be very confusing for loved ones to witness, especially if they're not used to having meltdowns themselves. Research into children with autism-related emotional regulation problems has shown that a higher level of parental involvement in therapy than is usual can be helpful[127]. Many adult women also find it helpful to enlist the help of a trusted partner or family member and when I'm working with women with autism, I find that if they have someone who can support them in this way it can be beneficial. Partners and family members can assist with emotional regulation and encourage their loved ones to put into place their new thoughts and actions, finding ways of helping them make the links between their more emotional brains and their "thinking" brains. You can educate those who are close to you by explaining to them that this has always been part of your emotional response and that, whilst it may look extreme to them, this is part of your autism. Explain that you become overwhelmed, confused, overloaded, frustrated and trapped (or whatever your particular experience is), and that these feelings can lead to you having a meltdown. Explain that, even though the situation which has triggered the meltdown may seem fairly minor, to you it was confusing and overwhelming – because of the way your brain works. Understanding that your meltdowns are caused by your autism is a useful step for both you and people close to you in normalising them. They may not be pleasant to experience, and you can work on developing more helpful emotional regulation strategies, but they are commonly experienced by women with autism.

My partner used to find my meltdowns quite disturbing to be around. Now, he knows it is part of a process that I go through when I am feeling stressed. This doesn't downplay the fact that

I am genuinely upset, confused and completely overwhelmed in the moment, but it does help him to understand that, bad as it might look, it will pass and I will be back to my usual self in a comparatively short space of time. We also both now know what is likely to trigger a meltdown. If I am in a situation where I feel stressed, such as having to present a new course to a group, it's pretty much guaranteed the night before I am going to end up crying and angry at some point. Knowing that this is probably going to happen, and having my partner on hand to offer the right type of support, helps me diffuse the situation far more quickly than I would have been able to in the past.

The "right type" of support is critical here and it's useful to explain to people close to you what you need in that type of situation. If they offer the wrong kind of support, they can make the situation far worse. For instance, if someone tells you that "it'll be fine, you've nothing to worry about", or "you always get like this, don't you", and that's not what you need, you might find yourself spiralling into a far worse state. In addition to explaining what a meltdown feels like, it is useful to explain what you need from your partner/ family member during, and following, a meltdown. Some people find that being asked questions about why they're upset or having someone trying to find solutions to the problem can be extremely frustrating and simply something that they cannot understand at that moment, no matter how well meaning. What works for me is being listened to, with very little input, and being told, in very simple language, that I am good at what I do. If my partner tries to hold a more detailed conversation, I'm liable to verbally lash out. What works for you may be something quite different and it is important to have a conversation with those close to you, when you are in a calm state, about how they can best help you when you are feeling highly emotional.

Angela told me, "My partner knows now she has to just hold me. If she tries to talk things through with me, I just get more and more wound up. I just need held close".

Tonya described what she needed from her partner as, "space and patience. He used to try and get me to explain how I was feeling and we'd sometimes fall out because I couldn't communicate in that way, which made him feel excluded. Now he knows I'm not excluding him but I literally can't engage with his process of trying to come up with solutions".

Exercise:

Write down what you need from those close to you when you are feeling stressed or worried, or when you are recovering from a meltdown. How can you explain what a meltdown feels like? What can you ask your friend, partner or family member to do before or after a meltdown?

The emotional regulation timeline & mindfulness

It's also useful for both you, and those close to you, to be aware that there is a "timeline" when it comes to emotional regulation and to find out what might be helpful at particular points on that timeline, including noticing when you're in the early stages of distress by being aware of actions like pacing, rocking, not answering, avoidance or hyperactivity[128]. During these early stages, it can be important to take a break, divert attention or redirect what you're doing and this is a good time to ensure you've had a discussion with those close to you about what may or may not be helpful. It's also important for both you and people around you to be aware that it can take you a long time to calm down and return to your emotional baseline[129].

Mindfulness is an emotional regulation strategy which can be very helpful to people with autism. To become more mindful involves learning how to accept what you are feeling without judgement. It involves accepting your thoughts for what they are. Just thoughts. When you become aware that all thoughts shift and change and are never constant, you can begin to realise that your thoughts, no matter how significant they feel to you at the time, do not control you. They will pass and, through adopting a more mindful attitude, you can begin to choose where to direct your attention with regards to how much attention you give to your thoughts. Learning to accept our thoughts in this way allows us to become more aware of the types of emotions, without getting so caught up in them, in their earliest stages. When we become aware in this way, we can focus on slowing down, accepting that the way we are thinking and feeling is part of our process of emotional regulation, and so avoid a situation where we are trying to escape or suppress an emotional meltdown[130].

Maureen noted that she found it easier to avoid a full meltdown by employing the timeline concept and recognising her emotional state in the earlier stages. "I recognise now that I'll start feeling quite withdrawn and uncommunicative if a meltdown is brewing, often in relation to something stressful which is coming up at work".

Jada noticed that her pre-warning signals included pacing and stimming, including starting to rub her feet together a lot. "I find myself having to do things with my body long before I know how distressed I'm becoming. I'll pace and sit, sometimes very still, rubbing my feet together. I know now that these are signs that I'm very stressed and might be heading for a meltdown if something triggers it".

Diana described how important it was to have recovery time after a meltdown. "When I have a meltdown, it really takes it out of me. I can't be rushed out of it. I have to go and lie in a dark room and probably fall asleep before I can really get over it. I have to be on my own".

Once you have identified your own personal emotional regulation timeline, you can develop strategies to help manage it. For instance, if you know that you are more prone to meltdowns if you are tired or hungry, it is important to come up with a plan to ensure you have a good sleep and have eaten properly, particularly if you know you're going into a potentially triggering situation. It's also crucial to identify what those triggering situations are and to realise that the situation itself is probably never going to feel much better for you. What you can work on, is preparing for how you will be in that situation and have strategies to cope if it becomes too difficult. For instance, if you know that going to the supermarket is likely to trigger extreme stress and sensory overload, can you make sure you go at a time of day when you're feeling more refreshed an energised? Or could you shift to online deliveries? If you're already feeling slightly stressed, is it possible to avoid taking on something which could dramatically increase those stress levels? If you are noticing any of the behaviours which might signify the early stages of emotional dysregulation, such as pacing, humming, talking to yourself, pouring yourself into work, stimming more than usual or moving in a hurried way, can you take some time out to rest? It can be useful to keep a journal, noticing your mood at particular times of day (even if it just involves drawing a smiley/ sad/ angry face to represent how you feel at a given time) so that you can develop an awareness of where you might be on your emotional regulation timeline and what steps you can take to help yourself.

Exercise:

Think about the type of situations which sometimes culminates in a meltdown.

Take some time and think about a phrase or word which would help you feel more relaxed and in control in that type of situation. You could use or adapt the sentences from above and other suggestions include:

I am safe

I can get through this

I can call on support

Alternatively, is there an object – such as a smooth stone or soft piece of material – which could comfort you in that type of situation? Or there might be a scent – such as a perfume or essential oil – which has calming properties for you. If so, get the object or the scent, and touch or breathe it in, repeating to yourself that you are safe and in control.

Whatever you have set up as your "anchor", whether it's a word, phrase, scent or object, you can take that with you and focus all your attention on it the next time you feel that things are spiraling. It is especially useful when you're out and about and need to cope with the situation until you reach a safe, quiet place or can access the support of someone who can help.

13 MAKING SENSE OF THE PAST

Our past informs our present and who we currently are is a sum of all our experiences to date. Many people face issues moving forwards in life because they cannot recognise the links between their current ways of thinking and acting and what has happened in their past. They may also face problems if they have confronted difficulties in their past which they have not come to terms with. When you have experienced trauma in the past, it can affect your sense of self-identity and self-esteem. In contrast to realising that there is an explanation, rooted in your past, for the ways you think and act, you may turn it in on yourself and come to the conclusion that you are somehow flawed as a person.

Making sense of your past – and bringing your adult diagnosis of autism into that endeavour – is an essential part of learning about who you are. You may have experienced things which have haunted you over the years and past experiences which cause you continuing embarrassment and shame. You may feel judgemental and angry towards your younger self for the way you dealt with a particular person or situation. You may carry regret that you did or did not pursue a particular course of action. When you revisit these experiences through the lens of someone who had undiagnosed autism, you may find yourself looking back with a far healthier perspective[131].

Autism or not, there is nothing positive to be gained from self-blame and self-dislike. We are all quick to be our harshest critics and all that achieves is to make us feel bad about ourselves. We might ending up drinking, experiencing eating disorders, taking drugs, over-working or lashing out at people in an attempt to dull the pain we carry. Exploring our pasts is not an exercise in absolving personal responsibility. It is an exercise in self-growth and self-development.

In addition to shedding clarity on some of the difficulties we have experienced in our pasts, our post-autism-diagnosis perspective allows us to recognise our strengths. Instead of being harsh on ourself for not being the most popular girl in school, we can consider how well we did to make and maintain any friends at all. In contrast to putting ourself down for having interests which other people thought were strange, we can be proud of ourself for having been different and having been interested in subjects which contributed to who we are. By revisiting your past, in addition to recognising the hardships you faced, you can become aware of your strengths and determination and unique set of qualities which you have displayed throughout your whole life. One study showed that women who considered themselves successful noted that their experience in overcoming obstacles in their lives had helped them to become more efficient and had been instrumental in shaping their success[132]. Reviewing your past through this lens can be an extremely empowering and motivating experience.

I had always been very judgemental of my younger self. Why did I let myself be bullied? Why did I wander about with a spelling book? Why was I so unbelievably shy? Why did I try to come first in everything when I should have been playing and having fun? Why did I suffer for months with a little lump on my skin, which I thought was cancer, and not tell anyone because the thought of the attention it would attract was too overwhelming for me? As an adult looking back, I used to feel annoyed and ashamed of my younger self.

Revisiting and reviewing my past, from the perspective of someone with autism, helped me to see that I was an unbelievably strong little girl who did her best to cope with a pretty rubbish situation. I still showed up to school, despite the migraines and the bullying. I still put effort into being as sociable as I could, despite the feelings of sickness and confusion when people spoke to me. Instead of seeing myself as a strange, pathetic child, I began to see myself as a precious child who had kept on trying to do her best and who struggled through so that I could become the person I am today.

Marianne experienced a similar re-evaluation of herself as a child and teenager when she looked at her experiences through her post-autism lens. "I've spent my whole life really hating myself deep down. I've had problems with alcohol and self-harming. I couldn't even bear to think of myself as a kid without being really embarrassed, and I carried that embarrassment with me. It's been so useful to spend some time reviewing what happened, now that I know about my autism. I can see that I did pretty well given the circumstances".

Jo told me, "I could never understand why I was such a weird child. I've basically spent my whole life feeling weird and different. I tried not to think about what life was like when I was younger, but if I did, I just felt a bit disgusted with myself. Now, I can see that I was actually a really strong child. I was going through hell, with no support, but I kept trying and I got through school and went to university. I'm proud of that resilience now".

Jane told me that she had always struggled with depression and anxiety and had attempted suicide when she was younger. "I've built up my own business and I'm in a relationship, which are both things I could never have imagined. I've always been hard on myself, thinking the business could be more successful and wondering why I cause my partner so much grief with my meltdowns. Since my diagnosis, I've turned this around. I think I'm pretty amazing achieving what I have with all my past difficulties!".

Maureen told me, "I feel like I'm pretty tough. I've had to fight my corner so often and I've overcome a history of abuse. I used to be very easily led and I've overcome that tendency but it's taken a huge amount of effort. That toughness I've got, and the things I've come through in my past, have made me the strong person I am today".

Validation

One of most significant aspects of diagnosis for so many women is validation. To validate means to "demonstrate or support the truth or value of". Stop and think about that for a moment. To discover you have autism means that your lived experience, your inner knowledge of the struggles you have faced and the abilities you have, is supported as true. Imagine how this feels after a lifetime of facing criticism and being told – either directly or through the actions of others – that you are over-reactive and just need to make more of an effort to fit in and "be normal". Finally, you can turn round and say, "but I couldn't have fitted in and been normal! My brain is *actually different* to most people!". One study showed that some women had a sense of increased pride and confidence post-diagnosis, particularly when they received support from other women with autism[133].

So many women have struggled their entire lives and have been ignored or faced criticism if they have sought out help. Far from having their experiences validated, they are told that they are over-reacting, highly sensitive or too dramatic. Essentially, they are told that they are "wrong". Heather told me, "I tried. I *used* to try. Even as a teenager I just knew that things were hard for me. I knew I was different to other people and I tried to explain this to my parents. I tried to find help. But I was just told I was a bit dramatic or highly sensitive and I needed to grow up and get on with it".

Many women find it impossible to ask for help, unable to find the language to express what is wrong or to have the confidence that someone understanding and capable of listening to them is out there. Instead, they may communicate their troubles in a variety of unconscious ways, such as illness, having meltdowns, rebelliousness, withdrawing or through self-destructive behaviour.

When you've spent your whole seeking help, in one way or another, when you've had a sense that you really do see the world differently to other people and find it almost impossible to fit into the world generally and when you simply feel overwhelmed on a regular basis, the relief at being told that yes – your brain *does* work in a different way to most people – is immense. That sense of validation is such an integral part of the healing process for so many women in terms of self-esteem and self-acceptance.

Whether people have chosen to self-diagnose or have received a psychiatric diagnosis, I always ask them what their diagnosis means to them.

Melanie told me, "I feel like sticking my fingers up to all the people who told me to get on with it! I'm like, ha, I *knew* there was something going on with me and now I've got the opinion of an expert to support that!".

Jules explained, "I feel validated. That's the best word for it. My experiences – which go back my whole life – have been listened to and given a name. I just feel I have that validation that I was looking for".

For Carys, having her experience validated was important with regard to how she felt she would proceed with her life. "I've struggled over whether or not to share my diagnosis but actually I've spent so long being put down by people in my family and called weird because I need things to be a certain way that I've decided I do want to share it. I feel validated now that I have my diagnosis and although I don't want an apology, it means I can clearly state my case to people who thought I was just an over-reactive person".

Empathy for your younger self

Up until the point they become aware that they have autism, many women have low self-esteem and are highly self-judgemental which is often at the root of anxiety, depression and self-destructive behaviours. Who wants to be different as a child or teenager? Who wants to be confused, overwhelmed and tongue tied when other people are comfortably having fun? Until they have explored the possibility that they may have autism, and have come to terms with the impact that this has had on their entire lives, many women report a sense of dislike and disconnect for their younger selves which they carry on into adulthood in terms of low self-esteem.

Making sense of the past involves connecting with one's younger self and offering her the reassurance that she was right. She did find things difficult. Instead of feeling embarrassed and ashamed of some of the "weird" things you did when you were younger, you can begin to accept that you thought and acted in those ways because you are a certain way. You can begin to view your younger self as someone who needed love and care and attention to help her navigate a difficult world. Once you can begin to accept and be empathic towards your younger self, you can begin to take that acceptance and awareness to your adult self.

Jo told me that, "realising I had autism just gave me a whole new take on my childhood. I'd always felt sort of embarrassed and ashamed of myself. I struggled growing up. I was awkward socially and I felt different from other people, especially girls. I didn't even like thinking about what I'd been like as a child and teenager, but I began to feel sorry for my younger self and felt some compassion towards her".

Maureen had experienced extreme self-judgement towards herself as an adult, which was rooted in the self-judgement she had experienced in her teenage years. "I genuinely hated myself as a teenager. I couldn't understand why I was left out of stuff. I couldn't understand why I tried my best but I still seemed to do the wrong thing. I really hated thinking of those years until very recently. I was disgusted with the way I looked and acted and annoyed that I'd been so obviously strange. I've started to accept who I was back then and to realise there was a reason for that. That's been great in helping me be less judgemental towards myself now".

Carys described her childhood as, "confused and scary. I was this terrified little thing, this anxious teenager and although things have improved for me as an adult, I still couldn't work out why I was like that as a child. When I looked back, I felt like I must have done something wrong and that made me feel bad well into adulthood. Now, I know there was a reason that I was like that and it's made me feel much more comfortable in my current skin".

Reinterpreting trauma

When we have experienced trauma in our past, it tends to have lasting effects. People who have experienced Adverse Childhood Experiences (ACEs) are far more likely to experience chronic illness, depression, obesity, anxiety, suicide and addictions[134]. The link is clear but many people who have suffered trauma in their past – and who are still suffering as a result in their present – don't know that they have experienced trauma. Although some of my clients have experienced clearly identifiable trauma, others haven't been sexually or physically abused, had alcoholic parents, lived in poverty or experienced any of the other traumatic experiences that we tend to think of when we hear the word "trauma". But growing up with a brain which works differently to other people's and struggling with the most basic aspects of life can produce constant stress, anxiety and, ultimately, complex trauma.

Consider how traumatic it is to go to school every day and be in a constant state of fear and confusion. To feel confused and isolated during teenage years. To struggle in the workplace and feel unable to make women friends. This is what daily life can look like for a woman with autism. All of these experiences can add up to an experience of trauma, with or without the addition of more easily identifiable traumatic experiences.

Angela related how she always carried a rucksack full of books around with her, which caused some of the other kids to make fun of her. "One day this nice girl explained to me that it made me look weird, carrying this huge rucksack. She said that if I just put my books in the locker like everyone else, it would be ok. But I was worried about the whole process of putting them in the locker. I worried I would forget the number for it and I'd lose my books, so I kept carrying them round with me".

Diana told me that, whilst she was ok academically, she often found she couldn't concentrate in class which would end up affecting her grades and that she would often end up getting into trouble from her teachers. "I liked the lessons at school. Really enjoyed learning, but the rest of school was a nightmare. I always seemed to say something wrong or that other kids thought was funny and then I'd panic and couldn't concentrate in class so I'd get into trouble. I suffered extreme anxiety and became really depressed towards the end of school".

Jo described self-harming behaviours, from the age of 15. "I began cutting myself. I didn't know how else to handle the situation. I felt so out of place and alone and cutting myself was the only relief I got".

Abuse

Research shows that women with autism are more likely to experience abuse than the general female population, demonstrating a clear link between abuse and autism[135]. They are more likely to have been sexually, physically and emotionally abused, mugged and pressured into sexual contact[136]. It's easy to understand why girls and women with autism are more at risk of abuse, given their difficulties with social communication and cognitive empathy. When you have problems reading facial and body language, combined with a difficulty reading the subtext and working out other people's intentions, you are in a position where you can be easily manipulated by others into situations which can make you vulnerable to abusive behaviours. The lack of "fitting in" with their contemporaries and desire to form intense, close relationships with others, including people who would potentially exploit them, increases girls' risk for being abused and these are exactly the types of qualities that abusers may target[137].

Tonya described how, "I was so lonely. In high school, I

didn't have any female friends. When this older guy started showing me interest, I was a sitting duck. I realise now that he was grooming me from the start but I just liked that he liked me. It didn't dawn on me what he was doing and by the time we had sex together I was too deep in – and I thought he really loved me".

Jada told me how she now realised she had suffered emotional abuse at the hands of her mother for many years. "My mother was a narcissist, I know that now, and out of all my siblings she acted in an abusive way towards me. She gaslighted me, she had no respect for my boundaries growing up, she manipulated me to take care of her. I could never work out why I seemed to be the only one of six to be used in this way but it was because of my autism. I never realised that the way she acted was manipulative and controlling. My brothers and sisters saw her for what she was much earlier than I did and they had as little as possible to do with her, but I just took her at face value".

Maureen describes how, in her early adulthood, she was in a series of abusive relationships. "I always seemed to end up with the same kind of guy. He would be outgoing and controlling, which worked for me in the beginning because it meant he could take charge when we were out and take charge of decisions which would overwhelm me. Then these men would start controlling me and I never knew it had happened until it got to the point where I had my phone taken off me or I wasn't allowed to have a social life. Friends would tell me my latest boyfriend was no good, but I kept on repeating the same patterns until I got therapy".

14 YOUR AUTISM SUPERPOWERS

So far we've established that, particularly when it comes to growing up, life tends to be far harder for women with autism. Often, whilst growing up, the goal is simply to pass as "normal" and to be like other people, especially other females. Whilst this is completely understandable, not only can "masking" lead to the types of mental health issues identified above, it can also be limiting in terms of downplaying and denying the unique way your autistic brain works. Masking your true, authentic self means you're missing out on something which is really worth cultivating. Your autism superpowers.

People with autism have brains which operate differently to the majority of people. And this tends to give you advantages in several areas. Without having to be in the same league as someone who we might think of as a "genius", or with a talent which is absolutely extraordinary, you might have strengths in particular areas. Simply viewing the world in a different way, and having the ability to make connections which might be unavailable to neurotypical people, can give you an advantage in many areas. Many people come to view their autism in a positive light and one research study into high-functioning adults with autism showed that they were proud to have autism and did not want to be a neurotypical[138].

Restriction of interests & focus

People with autism often have "highly restricted, fixated interests that are abnormal in intensity or focus (such as strong attachment to or preoccupation with unusual objects, excessively circumscribed or perseverative interests)"[139]. The ability of people with autism to focus so intently on one subject, often to the exclusion of other things, can be a fantastic skill in so many areas of life, such as conducting research, design and technology. Any subject where an intense level of interest and focus is required is so well suited to people with autism.

Charlie described how her ability to focus exclusively on one subject had helped her academically. "I remember being in first year at university, where we had to take three subjects, and a third year student telling me how hard it was in third year. I just found it so much easier the further I got on because I could get so into a subject. I've been researching the same period in history now since my Ph.D., over ten years ago, and I'm still as obsessed with it".

Melanie described her ability to go deeply into a subject to the exclusion of everything else as being, "rubbish when it comes to ruminating on my personal life and going over things

I've done wrong, but brilliant when it comes to my work which requires me to make links and focus very intently for hours at a time".

Organisation and structure

Many people with autism have a need for structure, routine and organisation and without that, they can easily feel overwhelmed. Having order, structure and routines isn't a luxury – it's vital to mental wellbeing. A lifetime of creating order in this way is a great skill, from anything to always being on time to always completing work tasks on schedule. Like many of my clients, I have no concept of leaving things to the last minute. If I have a report to do, it'll be done ahead of schedule. If it was left to the last minute…it would be very unlikely to be done as I'd be too overwhelmed to do it.

Jada described her need for organisation as, "extremely useful. I've always needed things to be organised. If they're not, I feel ill. But this comes in really handy for having everything done well in advance when we're going on holiday, for instance. I'm responsible for managing a large department at work and the feedback I've got is that I've put really good organisational systems in place since I've been in this position".

Evie told me that she created structure by being able to see links which were different to those other people noticed. "I discovered a long time ago, when I was writing actually, that I come to the end point through a different route from most other people. I've used that same way of linking up tasks to create a great structure for how I work and it seems to be highly efficient".

Defending a cause

Many women with autism feel strongly drawn to particular causes. Combining their passion and special interests, with a sense of valuing individuality and a tendency towards black and white thinking, they often speak up where others are afraid to and become advocates and campaigners. These skills can emerge anywhere, from sticking up for a fellow pupil who is being bullied at school to defending a work colleague to speaking out about causes with a world-wide relevance. Whilst the need to speak out against perceived injustices doesn't always make life easy, the fact that you're prepared to put your neck on the line to defend a person or cause is something you should be proud of.

Affinity with animals

I should start off by saying that not all people with autism like animals (I know some who positively don't). However, many people with autism do have a very strong affinity with animals. Temple Grandin, professor of animal science at Colorado State University explains her affinity with animals as being due to the fact that she thinks in pictures in a similar way to animals, and because of an ability to communicate with animals on a non-verbal level[140]. Research into children with autism and animals has demonstrated the positive effect that interaction with animals can have on developmental aspects such as social interaction[141]. Personally, I have a strong affinity with animals and would rather spend time with my three cats than the vast majority of humans I know!

Margaret, a woman in her fifties who had autism told me that, "Animals have always been so accepting of me. I can sit with my cat for hours, just quiet. It's like I know what she's thinking".

So many of my clients have described to me a close affinity with animals, which they have been aware of since childhood. They often tell me about that feeling of going inwards which animals seem to respond well to, and a sense of connecting and "knowing" what is going on for animals.

Attention to detail

People with autism often have a very strong eye for detail and an ability to find patterns and anomalies. Combined with an ability to focus intently and perform high-quality, repetitive tasks, they are in demand by some companies, particularly in the information and technology sector. Microsoft started a programme in 2015 to hire people with autism and tech companies HP and New Relic, amongst others, have followed suit.

Diana told me, "I seem to see things that other people just

miss. I'll go into a room and notice straight away if anything is the least bit different. I notice patterns in things, like road signs. And this ability is so important in my work as a lab assistant".

Ella described her attention to detail as, "crucial to the industry I work in. I need to be able to sit for hours in front of a screen, noticing any anomalies. And I enjoy that".

Sensory awareness & creativity

People with autism experience the world in a different sensory way to neurotypical people. Whilst this can be overwhelming and sounds, scents and touch can quickly ruin a day out (I can't tell you how often I've had to leave a room if someone scratches their plate), it can also enrich life and lead to creative expression based on sensory richness. One study showed that people with autistic traits may have less quantity but greater quality of creative ideas[142].

A high proportion of my clients are employed, or self-employed, in creative fields or find that expressing themselves creatively is crucial to their mental wellbeing.

Helen told me, "When I realised that I just couldn't work in an environment with other people, I felt like a failure. But it drove me to turn my art into a career and I couldn't be happier now having that outlet for my creativity".

Phoebe described her creative streak as, "Always there. I excelled at art at school and never had any doubt that I wanted to pursue a career as an artist".

As part of living with autism, it is important to focus on your strengths and explore those aspects of your **personality** which make you stand out and have particular strengths and abilities. As part of the process of becoming authentic, you can spend some time exploring what's great about having autism. What makes you unique? What abilities and perceptions do you have which tend to be inaccessible for other people? How can you begin to embrace these, after a lifetime of ignoring or hiding them?

From a personal perspective, I don't think I have any outstanding qualities but I do know that my autistic brain enables me to complete some tasks more efficiently than many people. I don't consider myself the most articulate person in the world, far from it, and part of this is undoubtedly due to social and communication difficulties as a result of autism. From a very early age, I realised that I was far better at communicating through writing than I was through talking. For me, writing flows in a way in which words will never do and this lack of ability in talking led me to hone my writing skills. When something is a struggle and you find something else which is enjoyable and natural, it's no surprise you spend time and effort on that activity.

Another area in which I do well is research. My brain loves researching. It thrives on going deeper and deeper into one subject, looking for obscure references and making the links. Research comes very naturally to me and whilst I'm not saying it's easy, I know that my brain is well suited to processing complex written information. This is in contrast to my experience of receiving verbal directions. When someone explains how to get to a house three streets away, I stare at them as if I'm interested and I genuinely have no idea what they are saying. I nod and smile but for all I'm taking in they could be talking in a completely different language.

With or without a diagnosis of autism, you probably reach a point in life where you can identify your skills. I knew I liked writing and research before receiving a diagnosis. But, for me, having a diagnosis somehow enhanced that knowledge and gave me a sense of pride in having a brain which was different to many people's. It doesn't mean that I think my brain is better in any way, but I like thinking that some of my skills are due to the way my brain is wired.

Marianne told me, "I've always been good at drawing, from about the age of three. I could just do it. And I loved it. I could never explain why it came so naturally to me but I think now having autism is probably a big part of it".

Anne described how having a diagnosis of autism helped her to appreciate and value her skills more than she had done in the past. "People would tell me how amazing I was at writing. I got good scores in school, I went through the academic system, I knew I could do this thing but I had such low self-esteem that I'd always pull myself up and question whether I really was any good. Finding out I had autism made me realise that my brain actually worked in a way which did give me an advantage in certain areas and helped boost my confidence".

Exercise:

Take a moment or two to imagine yourself as a superhero (you can look, dress and be the way you want to be!).

You're holding up a banner with your superhero powers on it. What does it say? It might be things that you're naturally talented at and it might contain personal qualities which make you unique.

Once you've finished imagining your superhero self, take a note of what was on the banner. If you want to come up with a name for your incredible you, go for it!

15 YOU'RE MORE THAN A DIAGNOSIS

As part of your journey towards authenticity, and an embracement of your autism, you need to remember one really important thing. You're more than your diagnosis. Although you have autism, who you are is made up of all your experiences since birth; it is influenced by the culture you were born into, your gender and how you were raised by your parents. Whether you were the oldest or youngest in your family, whether your mother was loving and accepting or emotionally unavailable and whether you were born into a family of doctors or a family of construction workers are all going to impact your life experience and who you have become.

The discovery that you have autism is very useful in explaining some things in your life, from the most mundane (why can't you wear high heels?) to the most significant (why were you left out of teenage groups and had a miserable time in college?). But it doesn't explain everything.

Having autism doesn't mean you're completely different to neurotypical people. You experience some things more intensely and you have less of an understanding of some things which come more naturally to people without autism, but there is still a huge crossover between you and everyone who does not have autism.

Everyone is a combination of their environment and the way they were born. We know that autism is a developmental disorder – that is, you are born with it and would have it no matter how or where you were raised. This is in contrast to other psychological conditions which have a more complex interplay between environment and genetics where, despite a genetic propensity for a condition, upbringing often appears to be integral in whether or not a condition will develop. If you have autism, you could be raised in the most understanding, loving, supportive environment imaginable and…you'll still have autism. In contrast, if you have a genetic leaning towards bipolar disorder, for instance, this condition might not be triggered if were raised in a loving, supportive and accepting environment.

Even though autism is biologically rooted, it's not the be all and end all. Many of my clients, when making sense of their thinking and behaviours, ask me, "Is that my autism?". The honest answer is, often, "maybe". However, it could also be due to the fact that your mother rejected you as a child. Or perhaps it's due to the fact you were bullied relentlessly at school. Or maybe it's because your father physically abused you. It's important to recognise what has happened in our lives and the impact this has had on us. If we have been treated badly by others, we need to recognise this as part of learning to avoid particular relationship patterns.

When you are moving towards greater authenticity, interpreting everything in your life as being a consequence of having autism could potentially be limiting. For instance, if you have an issue forming close relationships with other people and you have a history of childhood emotional abuse, interpreting this difficulty as being a symptom of your autism could limit you from moving forwards in a positive way. Let's imagine that you feel threatened and vulnerable when you start to become close to someone, which leads to you pulling away. This may be partly due to the fact that you have autism. It's could also be due to the fact that you were pushed away by your mother when you looked for affection or bullied by your father on a regular basis. If you attribute all of your social intimacy issues to autism, you are missing the opportunity to make the necessary links between your past and current experience. If you don't make these links, you may find yourself repeating the same patterns, for instance, by choosing people who are emotionally abusive. You may also feel that being uncomfortable with close social relationships is just something you have to accept, because of your autism and, in so doing, might prevent yourself from forming the types of relationships that could potentially enrich your life.

Close relationships are just an example of how your

responses and reactions may owe more to environmental factors than autism. Let's imagine you have difficulties in controlling your emotions during times of pressure whilst you're at work. This is partly due to your autism and issues with emotional regulation. But perhaps you were raised in a family where, every time you tried to offer an opinion, you were shut down and criticised. In working through this issue, in addition to dealing with emotional regulation strategies, it's important to acknowledge how your core beliefs around communication have been shaped.

Tonya told me, "I love having my autism diagnosis. It's helped me loads in terms of accepting myself, but I think at the beginning I was sort of like, 'oh, that's because I have autism!', and whilst it was useful, I started to realise that not *everything* was because I had autism. I also had an extremely disruptive and abusive upbringing and it was useful for me to continue to explore the impact that continued to have on me".

For Maureen, instead of being a positive in her life, she had started to turn her diagnosis in on herself. "I have a lot of issues with codependency, being raised by an alcoholic mother with mental health issues. I'd reached a point previously in therapy where I could identify where some of my issues came from and when I got the autism diagnosis, I began to swing the other way and think that I'd have had similar issues regardless of my upbringing. It was important for me to step back and realise that the issues I face now are a combination of my autism *and* my upbringing".

Autism makes you uniquely placed with regards to how you see the world and the skills and qualities you have in some areas and it's important to take ownership of the positives which come with autism. However, it's also crucial that you recognise the skills and qualities which you have developed due to your life experiences more generally. For instance, your autism may have given you an ability to focus in on details which makes you an incredible researcher, but the fact that you were raised with a strong work ethic and are part of a culture which places a high value on academic attainment also influences how successful you are in your job. Autism may influence some black and white thinking patterns which tend to make it important for you to decide what is right and what is wrong and stand up for what's right, but the fact that you experienced bullying in the playground also informs why it is so important for you to stick up for the underdog.

Anne highlights the importance of acknowledging who she is, with regards to her strengths, by drawing on *everything* which has led her to this point. "I feel so much better about myself since my diagnosis. It helped me to turn around what I thought was unacceptable into realising these things, the quirks, were what made me really good at my job and were really valuable to me. But it was also important for me to recognise that my years as a single mother have contributed to the strong person I am today".

Diana told me that it was important to sit with her diagnosis for a while, "because it's tempting to just put everything from now on down to autism, but I think that could take away from me a bit all the things I've learned and all the skills I've developed throughout my life".

Following the early stages of diagnosis, when there may be fear about what a life with autism is going to look like, it's particularly important to remember that you are more than a diagnosis. Whilst having a label can be incredibly empowering, it can be experienced as limiting.

Danielle told me, "When I was first diagnosed, I was a bit shocked. I thought, 'how do you live a life with autism? What's my career going to look like? Will I get married and have kids?'. I panicked. A couple of years on and I know that I'm the same person I was before the diagnosis – just a bit…better! I still have the same family, still like doing the same things, I've just incorporated the diagnosis into my life so I can manage things better".

For Angela, being diagnosed initially felt, "like a limitation. I had to wallow for a bit. I had the phrase, 'I'm autistic' going round and round in my head and I wasn't entirely comfortable with it. What's an autistic person like? Then I realised I was me. I had autism. But I still had all the rest of me too. It took a little while to not see the autism as the be all and end all".

The way in which autism fits into your life and experience will be as unique as the life you have led and the experiences you have had. I had already been through several years of therapy before being diagnosed with autism and had made links between some of the issues I had faced in adulthood with depression, anxiety and addictions and aspects of my upbringing. When I received a diagnosis of autism it was tempting to go, "Well that explains it all, then!". But it didn't. My childhood experiences, as being part of a family and culture, still contributed to my difficulties in adulthood. The way I made sense of this complex interplay between nature and nurture was to identify how my reactions to my situation were shaped by autism, rather than to say that my situation wasn't significant. For instance, it had long been confusing to me why I became my mother's rescuer. It was a puzzle to me why the rest of my siblings stood up to some of her unreasonable demands whereas I was always completely compliant. I realised that because I had autism, I was more easily managed and manipulated and fell into the role of codependent because I took things literally and never realised there might be a more complex social agenda at play. With this situation, and others, I saw how autism and environment had both shaped me.

16 ACCESSING SUPPORT

As with anyone who has experienced difficulties in life, you may find it beneficial to access support. Whilst there are some therapists and organisations who provide services for people with autism, it can be difficult to access the right level of support.

On receiving her diagnosis, Angela told me, "I realise now I was very naïve. I assumed that 'being autistic' would mean that I could access services through the NHS or something. Instead, I was told I'd have to wait at least 6 months to see a therapist and that they wouldn't be specially trained in working with people with autism".

Jenny described visiting an organisation which specialised in working with people with autism and found the therapeutic support she received as, "being at totally the wrong level. I hate using terms like high and low functioning, but it was geared towards people who struggled greatly with day-to-day living and it didn't meet what I'd call my 'higher', or more complex, needs".

Maureen's experience with a non-specialist therapist echoed

the experience of many other women. "I felt like I had to teach my therapist about autism, which meant that the therapy wasn't as useful as it could have been. She had a great difficulty accepting that I was autistic in the first place and still kept trying to find a trauma based explanation for things which I'd learned were due to my autism".

Josie described her previous experience of therapy as, "very frustrating. First off, my counsellor wouldn't just accept that I was different and tried to come up with an environmental explanation for everything. But she also kept asking me how I felt and I just couldn't come up with the words. It stressed me out greatly".

Given the propensity of mental health issues which autistic people experience, there is a real need for trained healthcare professionals. People with high-functioning autism not only face delay in diagnosis[143] and accessing treatment[144] but also have an increased risk of being initially misdiagnosed with a mental health problem[145]. They are also more likely to experience a lack of post-diagnostic support[146].

One of the themes which emerged from a recent study of level 1 adult autistic people's experience was that 'people like me don't get support'[147], with people falling through the gap and finding themselves in a Catch-22 situation. High-functioning women found that they did not qualify for support through the usual mental health channels because of their autism diagnosis, but because they did not have a comorbid learning disability, they did not qualify for autism related support. Another theme which emerged from this research (which was made up from a predominantly female sample) was that people were dismissed from accessing support because they were considered to be 'coping', 'functioning' or 'managing' for instance, if they lived independently and were in employment or full-time study[148]. The fact that support is often geared towards children, long waiting lists and a lack of funding also posed problems for high-functioning adults when it came to accessing support[149].

Another issue with regard to accessing the right type of specialist support, which has a proven track record in helping women reduce stress levels and improve functioning[150], is that some interventions actively encourage camouflaging behaviours which is linked with higher stress levels and increased mental health issues in women with autism[151]. Because of the association between camouflaging and mental health issues, it is important for clinicians who promote camouflaging efforts to explore whether these efforts are right for their patients in terms of values and manageability[152]. The right kind of support, on the other hand, created positive changes including improved self-esteem and self-awareness, acceptance, autonomy, social connections, self-understanding and an opening up of employment and educational opportunities[153].

Research showed that autistic adults experienced a lack of understanding and knowledge among professionals, including therapists' difficulties with "reading" people with autism[154]. Autistic people often find therapy difficult because of communication issues and being able to access the right words to describe their emotions. This can make it particularly hard for women with autism to engage with traditional psychotherapy where exploring emotions and awareness of the therapeutic relationship is fundamental to the therapeutic process. Some women reported camouflaging their symptoms during the therapeutic process in order to fit in with what they regarded as a social situation[155,156]. Given the fact that neurotypical adults face difficulties in interpreting autistic people's behaviour, and people with autism have difficult interpreting the behaviour of neurotypical adults[157], it's easy to see how misunderstandings can be an inherent part of non-specialist therapy.

Understanding what is happening during therapy and completing homework can be particularly difficult for adults with autism and, in order to benefit from a session, it may be helpful to work with therapist who incorporates autism-sensitive strategies including incorporating written and visual information into the session, taking breaks and thoroughly explaining therapy rules. You may also benefit from working with a therapist who understands the importance of using concrete language with you, emphasises behavioural change (rather than focusing on cognitive approaches) and is prepared to include a loved one in their work with you.

Fiona told me that her experience of working with me was quite different to her previous experiences of therapy. "I'm sure I saw some really good therapists, but they just didn't get me. It's so helpful to me that you understand that I simply see the world differently to other people. I can tell you about a situation where I reacted in a way I wasn't happy about and you take me through the various stages of my reaction and how that relates to autism. This has been so much more helpful than looking for the emotional roots of that reaction."

Tonya explained that, by being encouraged by previous therapists to explore the emotional roots of her communication issues, she failed to develop helpful strategies for dealing with her issues. "I was asked to tap into my emotions and explore what had led me to these emotional responses. I couldn't really find the roots. Now I realise I just have very intense emotional reactions because that's how my brain works. The work we've done together has helped me come up with strategies to control these emotions, which has felt far more empowering".

Shifting the emphasis from exploring *why* you experience such intense emotions to how can we work together to help you *manage* those intense emotions can be a welcome relief and incorporating techniques such as mindfulness based stress reduction can be extremely helpful for anxiety and depression symptoms, rumination and improving overall mood.

Applied Behavioural Analysis (ABA) is a widely used treatment for autism. This approach focuses on teaching skills including how to initiate communication and how to motivate oneself with regard to executive skills. This type of treatment will help people understand how and why humans use language to communicate and some find it helpful in developing strategies for more successful communication. ABA has come in for criticism from the autism community, however, for having misguided aims, encouraging camouflaging and for its rewards systems.

As with anyone who is seeking therapy, your individual needs will shape the form that therapy takes and it's important to find a therapist who understands the ways in which your autism affects you and the degree to which other life experiences have shaped you. When I'm working with clients, I have found that it is extremely important to them to recognise that autism is a significant part of their story. Even when they have experienced other significant inputs, including emotional abuse or neglect, it's useful to start from the fact that, in some respects, their brains work differently. In moving towards authenticity, you need to be aware of the fact that your brain works in a particular way which draws you to a particular behaviour. You can use this as your starting point to regain control of the situation.

Many of the strategies I help clients work through are focused on how to gain control over their emotional responses and recognising that some things may always require extra effort. For instance, if someone automatically responds, "yes" to every situation because they become confused when someone asks them to do something, I focus on helping them develop a "time out" strategy so that they can have some breathing space and respond once the confusion time has passed. In this way, I help a client to accept the confusion (or whatever else is happening for them in terms of how their brain is processing things in a given situation) as simply being there. We then find a way to deal with this issue at the level of "how shall we deal with your way of processing in this situation?".

Educating yourself about the way your brain works is an integral part of the therapeutic process for women with autism. If you can find a therapist who specialises in working with women with autism you will receive this level of education. Understanding why you feel things more intensely, why you struggle to understand social cues, why you suffer from burnout, take comments literally and why sensory overload makes day-to-day living difficult is a fundamental step in dealing with these issues.

Another difference between specialist autism therapy and, for instance, more generalised therapeutic approaches is that it will recognise that some things are always going to be extremely hard, if not impossible, for you. Cognitive Behavioural Therapy starts from a general assumption that, through changing your thoughts and beliefs about a situation and changing your behaviours in incremental steps, you can continue to develop coping strategies for situations which have been difficult and build on your progress. As a woman with autism, when you're working with a therapist, it is important that they are aware that some things will always be difficult for you – no matter how hard you push yourself. In fact, pushing yourself can be extremely detrimental to your mental health. This doesn't mean you need to limit yourself in any way, but it can mean that, instead of continuing to expose yourself to difficult situations in the hope that you'll become used to them, you might need to consider a change of direction.

Whilst any good therapist will ensure that they cover aspects of self-care with their clients, someone who specialises in working with autistic clients will understand the particular types of self-care needs of their clients. Women with autism need to be very aware of the fact that they may need more time on their own, more time for creative outlets and may have particular needs around sleeping and day-to-day life. A specialist therapist who specialises will be able to provide the right kind of support and direction for you to meet your self-care needs.

Rosa describes the contrast between receiving specialist help with her previous experience of therapy. "I was sent for CBT and I pushed myself incredibly hard. What the therapist said made total sense to me, but I ended up getting more and more stressed, pushing myself more and more and ultimately feeling like a total stranger. Now I know there are some things I shouldn't be pushing myself to do because it leads to complete burnout and it never gets any easier".

Whether you are seeking out help from a therapist who specialises in women's autism or a more general therapist, it is important to find someone with whom you feel comfortable, safe and listened to. It is also important to work with someone who is willing to acknowledge your autism, even if this is a new area to them, and who is willing to learn more about your condition. As our knowledge of autism increases, hopefully more therapists will be aware of the ways in which autism presents in women and will be more ready to incorporate neurodivergent experiences into their approaches.

17 GOING FORWARDS

As you have read and interacted with this book, you will have come to a greater understanding of autism and of how you can come to terms with having autism and leading a fulfilled, authentic life.

How you take that knowledge and experience forwards will depend on who you are as a person. It may take a while for all the information you have learned from reading this book, and conducting other personal research along the way, to sink in. You may be feeling excited or scared. Motivated or stuck. Relieved or confused. And all of these feelings are ok. There's no set timeline or one way to respond to the discovery that you have autism but you can now focus on how you take your growing sense of awareness forwards.

Whether you choose to go it alone and continue reading and researching the subject, join a support group or seek out therapeutic help, you're not alone. Awareness of the ways in which women are affected by autism is continually growing as is evident from the growing body of research in this area and the increasing number of women who are speaking out about their experiences. Particularly in the case of women who have reached adulthood without realising they were autistic, this is a positive time to join the growing number of women who are reclaiming their voice and experiencing the empowerment of being able to name their experience.

As you continue your journey, you'll probably notice more and more of your little "quirks" and aspects of your behaviour which you have always taken for granted as being "autistic" in nature. Some of these discoveries are quite amusing (it was about two years post-diagnosis that I realised my habit of rubbing my feet together was a form of stimming) and others provide yet another jigsaw piece which makes just a bit more sense of the puzzle of your life. Becoming more knowledgeable about yourself and your relationship with autism leads, over time, to a greater sense of self-acceptance and more confidence in your uniqueness. Those changes you make, from having more time alone, to preparing breakfast beforehand, to changing career, all add up over time to fostering a sense of valuing your needs and valuing yourself for who you are.

Whatever life stage you're at, this is an exciting point of transition which you can embrace softly and gently, or loud and proud, as you move towards the life you truly deserve.

REFERENCES

1. Hull, L, Mandy, W, Lai, M-C, Baron-Cohen, S, Allison, C, Smith, P, Petrides, KV (2019) 'Development and validation of the Camouflaging Autistic Traits Questionnaire (CAT-Q)', *Journal of Autism and Developmental Disorders*, 49(3), p819-833

2. American Psychiatric Association. (2013). *Diagnostic and statistical manual of mental disorders* (5th ed.) https://doi.org/10.1176/appi.books.9780890425596

3. Livingston, LA, Shah, P, Happe, F (2019) 'Compensatory strategies below the behavioural surface in autism: A qualitative study', *Lancet Psychiatry*, 6(9), p766-777

4. Lai, M-C, Lombardo, MV, Ruigrok, AN, Chakrabarti, B, Auyeung, B, Szatmari, P, Baron-Cohen, S (2017) 'Quantifying and exploring camouflaging in men and women with autism', *Autism*, 21, p690-702

5. Hull, L, Mandy, W, Lai, M-C, Baron-Cohen, S, Allison, C, Smith, P, Petrides, KV (2019) 'Development and validation of the Camouflaging Autistic Traits Questionnaire (CAT-Q)', *Journal of Autism and Developmental Disorders*, 49(3), p.819-833

6. Cage, E, Troxell-Whitman, Z (2019) 'Understanding the reasons, contexts and costs of camouflaging for autistic adults', *Journal of Autism and Developmental Disorders,* 49(5), p1899-1911

7. Lai, M-C, Kassee, C, Besney, R, Bonato, S, Hull, L, Mandy, W, Szatmari, P, Ameis, SH (2019) 'Prevalence of co-occurring mental health diagnoses in the autism population: A systematic review and meta-analysis', *Lancet Psychiatry*, 6(10), p819-829

8. American Psychiatric Association. (2013) *Diagnostic and statistical manual of mental disorders* (5th ed.) https://doi.org/10.1176/appi.books.9780890425596

9. Satterstrom, FK, Kosmicki, JA, Wang, J *et al.* (2020) 'Large-scale exome sequencing study implicates both developmental and functional changes in the neurobiology of autism', *Cell*, 180(3), p568–584.

10. Tick, B, Bolton, P, Happe, F *et al.* (2016) 'Heritabiliity of autism spectrum disorders: a meta-analysis of twin studies', *Journal of Child Psychology and Psychiatry*, 57(5), p585-595

11. Johnson, JG, Cohen, P, Karsen, S, Ehrensaft, MK, Crawford, TN (2006) 'Associations of parental personality disorders and axis 1 disorders with childrearing behaviour', *Psychiatry*, 69, p336-350

12. Roberts, AL, Koenen, KC, Lyall, K, Robinson, EB, Weiskopf, MC (2015) 'Association of autistic traits in adulthood with childhood abuse, interpersonal victimisation and posttraumatic stress', *Childhood Abuse and Neglect*, 45, p135-142

13. Roberts, AL, Lyall, K, Rich-Edwards, JW, Ascherio, A, Weisskopf, MG (2013) 'Maternal exposure to childhood abuse is association with elevated risk of autism', *JAMA Psychiatry*, 70(5), p508-515

14. Liu, D, Caldji, C, Sharma, S, Plotsky, PM, Meaney, MJ (2000) 'Influence of neonatal rearing conditions on stress-induced adrenocorticotropin responses and norepinephrine release in the hypothalamic paraventricular nucleus', *Journal of Neuroendocrinologyl*, 12(1), p5-12

15. Heim, C, Nemeroff, CB (2001) 'The role of childhood trauma in the neurobiology of mood and anxiety disorders: preclinical and clinical studies', *Biological Psychiatry*, 49, p1023-1039

16. Brand, SR, Brennan, PA, Newport, DJ, Smith, AK, Weiss, T, Stowe, ZN (2010) 'The impact of maternal childhood abuse on material and

infant HPA axis function in the post-partum period',
Psychoneuroendrocrinology, 35, p686-93

17. Wadha, PD, Dunkel-Schetter, C, Chicz-De Met, A, Porto, M,
Sandman, CA (1996) 'Prenatal psychosocial factors and the
neuroendrocrine axis in human pregnancy', *Psychosomatic Medicine*, 58,
p432-446

18. Marinovic-Curin, J, Marinovic-Terzic, I, Byjas-Petkovic, J, Zekan, L,
Skrabi, E, Doga, Z, Terzic, J (2008) 'Slower cortisol response during
ACTH stimulation test in autistic children', *European Child and
Adolescent Psychiatry*, 17, p39-43

19. Slopen, N, Kubzansky, L, McLaughlin, K, Koenen, K (2012)
'Childhood adversity and inflammatory processes in youth: a
prospective study', *Psychoneuroendricrinology*

20. Ashdown, H, Dumont, Y, Ng, m, Poole, I, Boksa, P, Luheshi, GN
(2006) 'The role of cytokines in mediating effects of prenatal
infection on the fetus: implications for schizophrenia', *Molecular
Psychiatry*, 11, p47-55

21. Licinio, J, Alvarado, I, Wong, MC (2002) 'Autoimmunity in autism',
Molecular Psychiatry, 7, p329

22. Jonakai, GM (2007) 'The effects of maternal inflammation in
neuronal development: possible mechanisms', *International Journal of
Developmental Neuroscience*, 25, p415-25

23. Lennartsson, AK, Kushnir, MM, Bergquist, J, Billig, H, Johnsdottir,
IH (2012) 'Sex steroid levels temporarily increase in response to
acute psychosocial stress in healthy men and women', *International
Journal of Psychophysiology*, 84, p246-253

24. Vorocek, M (2010) 'Fetal androgens and autism', *The British Journal of
Psychiatry: The Journal of Mental Science*, 196, p416-417

25. Larsson, HJ, Eaton, WW, Masden, KM, Vertergaard, M, Olerson,
AV, Agerbo, E, Schedd, D, Thorsen, D, Martensen, PB (2005) 'Risk

factors for autism: perinatal factors, parents psychiatric history and socioeconomic status', *American Journal of Epidemiology*, 161, p916-925

26. Butbach, TPH, Van der Zwaag, B (2009) 'Contact in the genetics of autism and schizophrenia', *Trends in Neuroscience*, 32, p69-72

27. Daniels, JL, Forssen, U, Hultman, CM, Cnattingus, S, Santz, DA, Feychting, M, Sparen, P (2008) 'Parental psychiatric disorders associated with autism spectrum disorders in the offspring', *Pediatrics*, 121, e1357-1362

28. DeVilbiss, EA, Magnusson, C, Gardner, RM (2017) 'Antenatal nutritional supplementation and autism spectrum disorders in the Stockholm youth cohort: population based cohort study', *British Medical Journal*, 359;j4273

29. Kanner, L (1949) 'Problems of nosology and psychodynamics of early infantile autism', *American Journal of Orthopsychiatry*, 19, p416-426

30. Bettleheim, B (1967) *The empty fortress: infantile autism and the birth of the self*. New York: Free Press

31. Wing, L (1996) *The autistic spectrum: a guide for parents and professionals*. Constable

32. Bleuler E. (1950[1911]) *Dementia praecox or the group of schizophrenias*. New York: International Universities

33. Kanner L (1943) 'Autistic disturbances of affective contact', *The Nervous Child*, 2, p217–50

34. Asperger, H. (1944) 'Die 'Autistischen psychopathen im kindesalter', *Archiv für Psychiatrie und Nervenkrankenheiten*, 117, p76-136.

35. Baron-Cohen, S (2002) The extreme male brain theory of autism, *Trends in Cognitive Science*, 6(6) p248-54

36. Kopp, S & Gillberg, C (1992) Girls with social deficits and learning problems: autism, atypical Asperger syndrome or a variant of these conditions, *European Child & Adolescent Psychiatry*, 1(2), p89-99

37. Lai, MC, Lombardo, MV, Auyeung, B, Chakrabarti, B, Baron-Cohen, S (2015) Sex/ gender differences and autism: setting the scene for future research, *Journal of the American Academy of Child & Adolescent Psychiatry*, 54(1), p11-24

38. Brugha, TS, McManus, S, Bankart, J, Scott, F, Pardon, S, Smith, J, Bebbington, P, Jenkins, R, Meltzer, H (2011) Epidemiology of autism spectrum sisorders in adults in the community in England, *Archives of General Psychiatry*, 68(5), p459-465

39. Kim, YS, Leventhal, BL, Koh, YJ, Fombonne, E, Laska, E, Lim, EC, Song, DH (2011) Prevalence of autism spectrum disorders in a total population sample, *American Journal of Psychiatry*, 168(9), p904-912

40. Loomes, R, Hull, L, Mandy, WPL (2017) What is the male-to-female ratio in autism spectrum disorder: a systematic review and meta-analysis, *Journal of the American Academy of Child and Adolescent Psychiatry*, 56(6), p466-74

41. Lai, MC, Lombardo, MV, Pasco, G, Ruigrok, AN, Wheelwright, SJ & Sadek, SA (2011) A behavioural comparison of male and female adults with high-functioning autism spectrum conditions, *PLoS ONE*, 6(6), e20835

42. Gould, J & Ashton-Smith, J (2011) Missed diagnosis or misdiagnosis? Girls and women on the autism spectrum, *Good Autism Practice*, 12(1), p34-41

43. Ibid.

44. Pellicano, E, Dinsmore, A & Charman, T (2014) What should autism research focus on? Community views and priorities from the United Kingdom, *Autism*, 18(7), p756-770

45. Beck, JS, Lundwall, RZ, Gabrielsen, T, Cox, JC, South, M (2020) Looking good but feeling bad: "camouflaging" behaviours and mental health in women with autistic traits, *Autism*, 24(4), p809-821

46. Pellicano, E, Dinsmore, A & Charman, T (2014) What should autism research focus on? Community views and priorities from the United Kingdom, *Autism*, 18(7), p756-770

47. Lai, M-C, Lombardon, MV, Ruigrok, ANV, Chakrabarti, B, Auyeung, B, Szatmari, P. Happe, F, Baron-Cohen, S (2017) Quantifying and exploring camouflaging in men and women with autism, *Autism*, 21(6), p690-702

48. Ruble DN, Martin CL, Berenbaum SA. (2006) 'Gender development', in Eisenberg N (ed.) *Social, emotional, and personality development.* Hoboken, NJ: Wiley, p858–932

49. Blakemore JEO, Berenbaum SA, Liben LS. (2009) *Gender development.* New York: Psychology Press

50. Lutchmaya S, Baron-Cohen S, Ragatt P (2002) 'Foetal testosterone and eye contact in 12-month-old human infants', *Infant Behaviour and Development*, 25, p327–335

51. Hittelman, JH, Dickes R (1979) 'Sex differences in neonatal eye contact time', *Merrill Palmer Quarterly*, 25, p171–184

52. Eisenberg N, Fabes RA, Spinrad TL (2006) 'Prosocial development', in Eisenberg N (ed.) *Social, emotional, and personality development.* Hoboken, NJ: Wiley, p646–718

53. Barbu, S, Cabanes, G, Le Maner-Idrissi, G (2011) 'Boys and girls on the playground: sex differences in social development are not stable across early childhood', *PLoS ONE*, 6(1): e16407

54. Gurian, M, Henley, P, Trueman, T, & Ebrary, I (2001) *Boys and girls learn differently: A guide for teachers and parents.* San Francisco: Jossey-Bass

55. Kanfiszer, L, Davies, F, Collins, S (2017) '"I was just so different": The experiences of women diagnosed with an autism spectrum disorder in adulthood in relation to gender and social relationships', *Autism*, 21(6), p661-669

56. Bargiela, S, Steward, R, Mandy, W (2016) 'The experiences of late-diagnosed women with autism spectrum conditions: an investigation of the female autism phenotype', *Journal of Autism and Developmental Disorders*, 46(10), p3281-3294

57. Hickey, A, Crabtree, J, Stott, J (2018) '"Suddenly the first fifty years of my life made sense": experiences of older people with autism', *Autism*, 22(3), p357-367

58. Leedham, A, Thompson, A, Smith, R, Freeth, M (2020) '"I was exhausted trying to figure it out": The experiences of females receiving an autism diagnosis in middle to late adulthood', *Autism*, 24, p135-146

59. Webster, AA, Garvis, S (2017) 'The importance of critical life moments: An explorative study of successful women with autism spectrum disorder', *Autism*, 21(6), p670-677

60. Hurlbutt, K & Chalmers, L (2002) 'Adults with autism speak out: perceptions of their life experiences', *Focus on Autism and other Developmental Disabilities*, 17(2), p103-111

61. Begeer, S, Mandell, D, Wijnker-Homes, B, Venderbosch, S, Rem, D, Stekelenburg, F, Koot, HM (2013) 'Sex differences in the timing of identification among children and adults with autism spectrum disorders', *Journal of Autism and Developmental Disorders*, 43, p1151-1156

62. Leedham, A, Thompson, A, Smith, R, Freeth, M (2020) '"I was exhausted trying to figure it out": The experiences of females receiving an autism diagnosis in middle to late adulthood', *Autism*, 24, p135-146

63. Portway, SM, Johnson, B (2005) 'Do you know I have Asperger's syndrome? Risks of a non-obvious disability', *Health, Risk and Society*, 7(1), p73-83

64. Jones, L, Goddard, L, Hill, EL, Henry, LA, Crane, L (2014) 'Experiences of receiving a diagnosis of autism spectrum disorder: a survey of adults in the United Kingdom', *Journal of Autism and Developmental Disorders*, 44(12), p3033-3044

65. Hull, L, Mandy, W, Lai, M-C, Baron-Cohen, S, Allison, C, Smith, P, Petrides, KV (2019) Development and validation of the Camouflaging Autistic Traits Questionnaire (CAT-Q). *Journal of Autism and Developmental Disorders*, 49(3), p819-833

66. Beck, JS, Lundwall, RZ, Gabrielsen, T, Cox, JC, South, M (2020) 'Looking good but feeling bad: "camouflaging" behaviours and mental health in women with autistic traits', *Autism*, 24(4), p809-821

67. Parish-Morris, J, Liberman, MY, Cieri, C et al. (2017) 'Linguistic camouglage in girls with Autism Spectrum Disorder', *Molecular Autism*, Sep 30;8:48.doi: 10.1186/s13229-017-0164-6. eCollection 2017.

68. Ibid.

69. Beck, JS, Lundwall, RZ, Gabrielsen, T, Cox, JC, South, M (2020) 'Looking good but feeling bad: "camouflaging" behaviours and mental health in women with autistic traits', *Autism*, 24(4), p809-821

70. Hull, L, Petrides, KV, Allison, C, Smith, P, Baron-Cohen, S, Lai, M-C, Mandy, W (2017) '"Putting on my best normal": social camouflaging in adults with autism spectrum conditions', *Journal of Autism and Developmental Disorders*, 47(8), p2519-2534

71. Ibid.

72. Ibid.

73. Cassidy, S, Bradley, L, Shaw, R, Baron-Cohen, S (2018) 'Risk markers for suicidality in autistic adults', *Molecular Autism*, 9(1), Article 42

74. Hull, L, Lai, M-C, Baron-Cohen, S, Allison, C, Smith, P, Petrides, KV, Mandy, W (2020) 'Gender differences in self-reported

camouflaging in autistic and non-autistic adults', *Autism*, 24, p352-363

75. Schuck, RK, Flores, RE, Fung, LK (2019) 'Brief report: sex/ gender differences in symptomology and camouflaging in adults with autism spectrum disorder', *Journal of Autism and Developmental Disorders*, 49, p2597-2604

76. Hull, L, Petrides, KV, Allison, C, Smith, P, Baron-Cohen, S, Lai, M-C, Mandy, W (2017) '"Putting on my best normal": social camouflaging in adults with autism spectrum conditions', *Journal of Autism and Developmental Disorders*, 47(8), p2519-2534

77. Cage, E, Troxell-Whitman, Z (2019) 'Understanding the reasons, contexts and costs of camouflaging for autistic adults', *Journal of Autism and Developmental Disorders,* 49(5), p1899-1911

78. Milner, V, McIntosh, H, Colvert, E, Happe, F (2019) 'A qualitative exploration of the female expression of autism spectrum disorder (ASD)', *Journal of Autism and Developmental Disorders,* 49, p2389-2402

79. Beck, JS, Lundwall, RZ, Gabrielsen, T, Cox, JC, South, M (2020) 'Looking good but feeling bad: "Camouflaging" behaviours and mental health in women with autistic traits', *Autism*, 24(4), p809-821

80. Hull, L, Mandy, W, Lai, M-C, Baron-Cohen, S, Allison, C, Smith, P, Petrides, KV (2019) 'Development and validation of the Camouflaging Autistic Traits Questionnaire (CAT-Q)', *Journal of Autism and Developmental Disorders*, 49(3), p819-833

81. Beck, JS, Lundwall, RZ, Gabrielsen, T, Cox, JC, South, M (2020) 'Looking good but feeling bad: "camouflaging" behaviours and mental health in women with autistic traits', *Autism*, 24(4), p809-821

82. Tint, A, Weiss, JA, Lunsky, Y (2017) 'Identifying the clinical needs and patterns of health service use of adolescent girls and women with autism spectrum disorder', *Autism Research*, 10, p1558-1566

83. Mandy, W, Chilvers, R, Chowdhury, U, Salter, G, Seigal, A, Skuse, D (2012) 'Sex differences in autism spectrum disorder: Evidence from a large sample of children and adolescents', *Journal of Autism and Developmental Disorders*, 42(7), p1304-1313

84. Cassidy, S, Bradley, L, Shaw, R, Baron-Cohen, S (2018) 'Risk markers for suicidality in autistic adults', *Molecular Autism*, 9(1), Article 42

85. Ingersoll, B, Hambrick, DZ (2011) 'The relationship between the broader autism phenotype, child severity, and stress and depression in parents of children with autism spectrum disorders', *Research in Autism Spectrum Disorders*, 5(1), p337-344

86. Nylander, L, Axmon, A, Bjorne, P, Ahlstrom, G, Gillberg, C (2018) 'Older adults with autism spectrum disorders in Sweden: A register study of diagnoses, psychiatric care utilisation and psychotropic medication of 601 individual', *Journal of Autism and Developmental Disorders*, 48(9), p3076-3085

87. Bolton, PF, Pickles, A, Murphy, M, Rutter, M (1996) 'Autism affective and other psychiatric disorders: Patterns of familial aggregation', *Psychological Medicine*, 28(2), p385-395

88. Piven, J, Palmer, P (1999) 'Psychiatric disorder and the broad autism phenotype: Evidence from a family study of multiple-incidence autism families', *American Journal of Psychiatry*, 156(4), p557-563

89. Beck, JS, Lundwall, RZ, Gabrielsen, T, Cox, JC, South, M (2020) 'Looking good but feeling bad: "camouflaging" behaviours and mental health in women with autistic traits', *Autism*, 24(4), p809-821

90. Hull, L, Petrides, KV, Allison, C, Smith, P, Baron-Cohen, S, Lai, M-C, Mandy, W (2017) '"Putting on my best normal": Social camouflaging in adults with autism spectrum conditions. *Journal of Autism and Developmental Disorders*', 47(8), p2519-2534

91. Ibid.

92. Tierney, S, Burns, J & Kilbey, E (2016) 'Looking behind the mask: social coping strategies of girls on the autistic spectrum', *Research in Autism Spectrum Disorders*, 23, p73-83

93. Engstrom, I, Ekstrom, L, Emilsson, B (2003) 'Psychosocial functioning in a group of Swedish adults with Asperger syndrome or high-functioning autism', *Autism*, 7(1), p99-110

94. Howlin, P (2000) 'Outcome in adult life for more able individuals with autism or Asperger's syndrome', *Autism*, 4(1), p63-83

95. Beck, JS, Lundwall, RZ, Gabrielsen, T, Cox, JC, South, M (2020) 'Looking good but feeling bad: "camouflaging" behaviours and mental health in women with autistic traits', *Autism*, 24(4), p809-821

96. Ibid.

97. Cassidy, S, Bradley, L, Shaw, R, Baron-Cohen, S (2018) 'Risk markers for suicidality in autistic adults', *Molecular Autism*, 9(1), Article 42

98. Goffman, E (1959) *The presentation of self in everyday life*. Anchor

99. Horne, RM, Johnson, MD, Galambos, NL & Krahn, HJ (2017) 'Time, money or gender: Prediction of the division of labour across life stages', *Sex Roles,* 78, p731-743

100. Bargiela, S, Steward, R, Mandy, W (2016) 'The experiences of late-diagnosed women with autism spectrum conditions: an investigation of the female autism phenotype', *Journal of Autism and Developmental Disorders*, 46(10), p3281-3294

101. Ibid.

102. Gotham, K. Bishop, SL, Brunwasser, S, Lord, C (2014) 'Rumination and perceived impairment associated with depressive symptoms in a verbal adolescent-adult ASD sample', *Autism Research: Official Journal of the International Society for Autism Research*, 7(3), p381-391

103. Bargiela, S, Steward, R, Mandy, W (2016) 'The experiences of late-diagnosed women with autism spectrum conditions: an investigation

of the female autism phenotype', *Journal of Autism and Developmental Disorders*, 46(10), 3281-3294

104. Ibid.

105. Strang, JF, Kenworthy, L, Dominska, A et al. (2014) 'Increased gender variance in autism spectrum disorders and attention deficit hyperactivity disorder', *Archives of Sexual Behaviour,* 43(8), p1525-1533

106. Kristensen, Z & Broome, AZ (2015) 'Autistic traits in an internet sample of gender variant UK adults', *The International Journal of Transgenderism*, 16(4), p234-245

107. White, SW, Elias, R, Capriola-Hall, NN, Smith, IC, Conner, CM, Asselin, SB, Howling, P, Getzel, EE & Mazefsky, CA (2017) 'Development of a college transition and support program for students with autism spectrum disorder', *Journal of Autism and Developmental Disorders*, 47(10), p3072-3078

108. Bargiela, S, Steward, R, Mandy, W (2016) 'The experiences of late-diagnosed women with autism spectrum conditions: an investigation of the female autism phenotype', *Journal of Autism and Developmental Disorders*, 46(10), p3281-3294

109. Ibid.

110. Mazefsky, CA, Herrington, J, Siegel, M, Scafa, A, Maddox, BB, Scahill, L, White, SW (2013) 'The role of emotion regulation in Autism Spectrum Disorder', *Journal of the American Academy of Child and Adolescent Psychiatry*, 52(7), p679-688

111. Ibid.

112. Ibid.

113. Ibid.

114. Richney, JA, Damiano, CR, Sabatino, A, Rittenberg, A, Petty, C, Bizzell, J, Voyvodic, J, Heller, AS, Coffman, MC, Smoski, M, Davidson, RJ, Dichter, GS (2015) 'Neural mechanisms of emotion regulation in Autism

Spectrum Disorder', *Journal of Autism Developmental Disorder*, 45(11), p3409-23

115. Peters, S (2012) *The chimp paradox: the mind management programme to help you achieve success, confidence and happiness.* Vermillion

116. Guy, L, Souders, M, Bradstreet, L, DeLussey, C, Herrington, JD (2014) 'Brief report: emotion regulation and respiratory sinus arrhythmia in autism spectrum disorder', *Journal of Autism Dev Disorder*, 44(10), p2614-20

117. Mazefsky, CA, Borue, X, Day, TN, Minshew, NJ (2014) 'Emotion regulation patterns in adolescents with high-functioning autism spectrum disorder: comparison to typically developing adolescents and association with psychiatric symptoms', *Autism Research* 7(3), p344-54

118. Wilson, BJ, Berg, JL, Zurawski, ME, King, KA (2013) 'Autism and externalising behaviour: buffering effects of parental emotion coaching', *Research in Autism Spectrum Disorders*, 7(6), p767-776

119. Samson, AC, Jardan, AY, Podell, RW, Phillips, JM, Gross, JJ (2015) 'Emotional regulation in children and adolescents with autism spectrum disorder', *Autism Research*, 8(1), p9-18

120. Ting,V & Weiss, JA (2017) 'Emotion regulation and parent co-regulation in children with autism spectrum disorder', *Journal of Autism and Developmental Disorders*, 47(3), p680-689

121. Nader-Grosbois, N & S Mazzone (2014) 'Emotion regulation, personality and social adjustment in children with autism spectrum disorders', *Psychology*, 5, p15

122. Ashburner, J, Zivani, J, Rodger, S (2010) 'Surviving in the mainstream: capacity of children with autism spectrum disorders to perform academically and regulate their emotions and behaviour at school', *Research in Autism Spectrum Disorders*, 4(1), p18-27

123. White, SW, Elias, R, Capriola-Hall, NN, Smith, IC, Conner, CM, Asselin, SB, Howling, P, Getzel, EE & Mazefsky, CA (2017) 'Development of a college transition and support program for students with autism spectrum disorder', *Journal of Autism and Developmental Disorders*, 47(10), p3072-3078

124. Righi, G, Benevides, J, Mazefsky, C, Siegel, M, Sheinkopf, SJ, Morrow, EM (2017) 'Predictors of inpatient psychiatric hospitalisation for children and adolescents with autism spectrum disorder', *Journal of Autism and Developmental Disorders*, DOI:10, 1007/s10803-017-3154-9

125. Butwick, A, Langstrom, N, Larsson, H (2017) 'Increased risk for substance use-related problems in autism spectrum disorders: a population based cohort study', *Journal of Autism and Developmental Disorders*, 47(1), p80-89

126. Arnevik, EA & Helverschou. SB (2016) 'Autism Spectrum Disorder and co-curring substance abuse disorder – a systematic review', *Substance Abuse,* 10, p69-75

127. Mazefsky, CA, Herrington, J, Siegel, M, Scafa, A, Maddox, BB, Scahill, L, White, SW (2013) 'The role of emotion regulation in Autism Spectrum Disorder', *Journal of the American Academy of Child and Adolescent Psychiatry*, 52(7), p679-688

128. Ibid.

129. Ibid.

130. Ibid.

131. Hickey, A, Crabtree, J, Stott, J (2018) '"Suddenly the first fifty years of my life made sense": experiences of older people with autism', *Autism*, 22(3), p357-367

132. Webster, AA, Garvis, S (2017) 'The importance of critical life moments: An explorative study of successful women with autism spectrum disorder', *Autism*, 21(6), p670-6777

133. Bargiela, S, Steward, R, Mandy, W (2016) 'The experiences of late-diagnosed women with autism spectrum conditions: an investigation of the female autism phenotype', *Journal of Autism and Developmental Disorders*, 46(10), p3281-3294

134. *The Adverse Childhood Experiences (ACE) Study. Atlanta, Georgia: Centers for Disease Control and Prevention, National Center for Injury Prevention and Control, Division of Violence Prevention. May 2014.* Archived from the original on 27 December 2015

135. Roberts, AL, Koenen, KC, Lyall, K, Robinson, EB, Weiskopf, MC (2015) 'Association of autistic traits in adulthood with childhood abuse, interpersonal victimisation and posttraumatic stress', *Childhood Abuse and Neglect*, 45, p135-142

136. Ibid.

137. Ibid.

138. Hurlbutt, K, Chalmers, L (2002) 'Adults with autism speak out: Perceptions of their life experiences', *Focus on Autism and Other Developmental Disability*, 17(2), p103-111

139. American Psychiatric Association. (2013). *Diagnostic and statistical manual of mental disorders* (5th ed.)
https://doi.org/10.1176/appi.books.9780890425596

140. Grandin, T (2006) *Thinking in pictures.* Bloomsbury Publishing

141. O'Haire, M. (2017) 'Research on animal-assisted intervention and autism spectrum disorder', 2012-2015, *Applied Developmental Science,* 21(3) p200–216

142. Best, C., Arora, S, Porter, F, Dohert, M. (2015) 'The relationship between subthreshold autistic traits, ambiguous figure perception and divergent thinking', *Journal of Autism and Developmental Disorders*, 45, p4064-4073

143. Howlin, P & Asgharan, A (1999) 'The diagnosis of autism and Asperger's Syndrome: findings from a study of 770 families', *Developmental Medicine and Child Neurology*, 41(12), p834-9

144. Bowker A, D'Angelo NM, Hicks R, Wells K (2011) 'Treatments for autism: parental choices and perceptions of change', Journal of Autism and Developmental Disorder, 41(10), p1373–82.

145. Punshon, C., Skirrow, P., & Murphy, G. (2009). 'The not guilty verdict: Psychological reactions to a diagnosis of Asperger syndrome in adulthood', *Autism: The International Journal of Research and Practice, 13*(3), p265–283

146. Jones, L, Goddard, L, Hill, EL, Henry, LA, Crane, L (2014) 'Experiences of receiving a diagnosis of autism spectrum disorder: a survey of adults in the United Kingdom', *Journal of Autism and Developmental Disorders,* 44 (12), p3033-3044

147. Camm-Crosbie, L, Bradley, L, Shaw, R, Baron-Cohen, S, Cassidy, S (2019) '"People like me don't get support": autistic adults' experiences of support and treatment for mental health difficulties, self-injury and suicidality', *Autism*, 23, p1431-1441

148. Ibid.

149. Ibid.

150. Jones, L, Goddard, L, Hill, EL, Henry, LA, Crane, L (2014) 'Experiences of receiving a diagnosis of autism spectrum disorder: A survey of adults in the United Kingdom', *Journal of Autism and Developmental Disorders,* 44(12), p3033-3044

151. Beck, JS, Lundwall, RZ, Gabrielsen, T, Cox, JC, South, M (2020) 'Looking good but feeling bad: "camouflaging" behaviours and mental health in women with autistic traits', *Autism*, 24(4), p809-821

152. Camm-Crosbie, L, Bradley, L, Shaw, R, Baron-Cohen, S, Cassidy, S (2019) '"People like me don't get support": autistic adults'

experiences of support and treatment for mental health difficulties, self-injury and suicidality', *Autism*, 23, p1431-1441

153. Ibid.

154. Ibid.

155. Hull, L, Petrides, KV, Allison, C, Smith, P, Baron-Cohen, S, Lai, M-C, Mandy, W (2017) '"Putting on my best normal": social camouflaging in adults with autism spectrum conditions', *Journal of Autism and Developmental Disorders*, 47(8), p2519-2534

156. Lai, M-C, Lombardo, MV, Ruigrok, AN, Chakrabarti, B, Auyeung, B, Szatmari, P, Baron-Cohen, S (2017) 'Quantifying and exploring camouflaging in men and women with autism', *Autism*, 21, p690-702

157. Cassidy, S, Bradley, L, Shaw, R, Baron-Cohen, S (2018) 'Risk markers for suicidality in autistic adults', *Molecular Autism*, 9(1), Article 42

ABOUT THE AUTHOR

Dr. Claire Jack is an internationally renowned life coach who provides ADOS-2 autism assessments and specializes in assessing adult women. In addition to helping women with autism pursue authentic, meaningful lives, Claire writes extensively about her experiences as an autistic woman. She lives in the West Coast of Scotland and when she's not writing in her favourite coffee shops, she enjoys long walks by the beach, spending time with her partner and children and curling up with her three cats.

Claire is the author of *Women with Autism, Embracing Autistic Motherhood, Level 1 Autistic Teens: A solution-focused approach to parenting*, and *Raised by a Narcissist*.

www.autism-assessment-online.com

Made in United States
Troutdale, OR
04/22/2024

19364191R00126